Read What Others Are Saying About
How To Achieve Your
Million-Dollar Dreams At Any Age

"I have been in the self-improvement arena for many years and have worked worldwide with the best teachers, including Deepak Chopra and Dr. Wayne Dyer. Kris Vigue is one who has learned the powerful techniques of visualization and goal setting at an early age, and has taken these techniques and used them in his own unique way to become a success. This amazing young man is not only a real cutie but has written a profoundly insightful book. This book is a must for EVERY college and high school student!"

Michele Blood
Musivation
Author: Be A Magnet To Success System

"This book is one of the best how-to resources on the market today. Already a proven leader in sports and business, Kris Vigue shares the information you need to help you achieve your Million-Dollar Dreams. This is a must-have addition to everyone's success library."

Tim Coleman
Soccer Outreach International

"In the same amount of time it takes to watch a movie, any teen or young adult will gain a lifetime worth of inspiration to achieve their dreams by reading Kris's book. The tools and resources shared in each chapter are invaluable to any young individual embarking on their journey to success in life."

Cristina Delgado, Graduate Student

"Everything you need to know about how to reach your greatest success and highest achievements won't be learned in school! Kris Vigue, with the knowledge and techniques you can learn from his book, will take you a giant step toward your dreams."

Doug Bench, President
Science For Success Systems

"Inspirational and practical! Kris Vigue provides a new generation of entrepreneurs with the tools to turn their dreams into reality. A must reading for anyone who wants to amass a great fortune in a short period of time!"

H. Skip Weitzen, Author
Hypergrowth: Applying The Success Secrets
Of America's Fastest Growing Companies

"Congratulations on your new book, and best of luck with it."
Dave Littlefield, General Manager
Pittsburgh Pirates

"When dealing with Kris his sincerity comes across very strongly, which is difficult to find these days. It's nice doing business with someone you know you can trust."
Tom & Steve Banas, Business Associates
Pristine Cards

"When I recruited Kris, I saw a lot of potential. His injury was devastating, but I know he'll bounce back and be successful at whatever he does. This book is an example of what I mean."
Tom Riginos, Assistant Head Baseball Coach
Clemson University

"Kris and I played baseball together at Lake Mary High School. I have seen his inner drive both on and off the field. I am constantly amazed at his skills and achievements."
Kyle Bono
Boston Red Sox Minor League Pitcher

"I have been an Athlete Agent for professional athletes for over seven years, and I am impressed with Kris's ability to re-focus. After reading his book I must say that he has a true understanding of what it takes to achieve your million-dollar dreams."
Tom O'Connell, President
Legends Management Group

"How good you are is of little value. How good you desire to be is priceless. The true value you have to offer is that of constant improvement. This is what makes the difference. Kris Vigue has shared this vision in his youth. Everyone should look closely at this message."
Karl Schilling
Author: Fabulous Fortunes Through F.A.I.L.U.R.E.

"Kris is a fine young man. He is a person who is dependable, loyal and a leader among his teammates."
Dr. John Winkin, Director
Husson Sports Leadership Institute

"If more high school kids had Kris's values and work ethic, this world would be a better place now and in the future. Thanks for being such a great role model for the team."
Ed Nuss, Baseball Coach
Lake Mary High School

Luke,
Best of luck in achieving all your
million-dollar dreams!

Ken Vigue

How To Achieve Your Million-Dollar Dreams At Any Age!

Kris Vigue

POWER
Publications, Inc.

Dedication

To all those who pursue their
Million-Dollar Dreams!

Table of Contents

Acknowledgements

In one of my chapters I talk about the importance of having gratitude for the people in your life. I've always been fortunate to have a solid team behind me. First my parents, who have instilled in me the belief that anything is possible if you set your mind and heart to it. They have shown continued support for everything that I have ever done, and through their encouragement made this book possible. My grandparents, aunts and uncles have traveled thousands of miles over the years to watch my sporting events and cheer me on. Their support was, and is endless in all areas of my life. My sister has had to endure a lot due to me, like going to game after game, and even moving. While I'll always think of her as my little sister, she will also always be my friend.

There are countless other people who have helped me along the way, especially numerous coaches who believed in me and gave me a chance. Friends and business associates have been supportive and encouraging; and there are still many new relationships just developing. I thank you all.

Foreword

By: Pat Williams
Senior Vice President, Orlando Magic

Most people who know me know that I am a voracious reader. I read just about everything I can get my hands on. If you've heard me speak, you also know that I believe reading and learning are essential keys to success.

As a person who has been in the professional sports arena for over 40 years, I have come to respect those athletes who not only play the game but who also study it. The ability to read and assimilate information is something no one can take away from you.

This fall I will be coming out with my 35th book, *The Three Success Secrets of Shamgar.* I guess you could say I am trying to do my part to get more people to read. I wrote my first book when I was 34. When I heard that a fellow member of Orlando's Executive Sports Connection *(an organization for local business people and former professional athletes),* Kris Vigue, was coming out with his first book at age 21, I had to say I was impressed.

Kris moved to Florida his senior year of high school to play baseball with some of the best ballplayers in the country. He had a great year and was signed by a Division I college. In the fall of his freshman year he suffered a career ending injury. As a former professional baseball player myself, I can understand how losing a dream could really affect you. Kris could have thrown in the towel as so many athletes do when their career is cut short by injuries, but instead he decided that if he couldn't achieve one dream, he would try and achieve another.

In his book, *How To Achieve Your Million-Dollar Dreams At Any Age,* Kris describes steps young people can take to achieve their goals, whatever they may be. I'm sure we are going to be seeing a lot more from this young man. I'd recommend his book to anyone in high school or college, as it will certainly give them a head start on their future Million-Dollar Dreams.

Pat Williams
Senior Vice President
Orlando Magic

Introduction

"Success comes from having a dream and setting
tangible, realizable goals that enable you to
see your dreams to completion."
Rich DeVos

Everyone has dreams – from the little boy who dreams of becoming a fireman, to the recent college graduate who dreams of owning her own business, to the retired couple who dreams of wintering in sunny Florida. Dreams are a vital part of living at every age.

But people with million-dollar dreams go one step farther than just having a dream. They take their original dream, think BIGGER, and then create a set of goals that will help them to achieve that dream. You don't need to be age 50 to do this, or age 40, or even age 30. You can have million-dollar dreams at 20, or at any age. In fact, I bet if you asked some of the most successful people in the world when they started dreaming their million-dollar dreams, many of them would tell you it was in their early twenties, teens, or possibly even before that! Tiger Woods was four years old when he started dreaming about being the best golfer in the world. I can guess that Donald Trump, Malcolm Forbes, or Andrew Carnegie all dreamed of being successful millionaires long before they were 25, too.

Just like there are no two snowflakes exactly the same, there are no two people exactly the same. Every person on this earth has his or her own set of special abilities and talents. Because of this I believe we are all capable of having our own unique million-dollar dreams. But unfortunately many people will never achieve those dreams because they will never take the time to conceive or imagine them. If you are reading this book, however, I'd say you are not one of those people and are ready to conceive, pursue and achieve your dreams.

Achieving your million-dollar dreams, however, will take more than simply having them—even though that's a step ahead of many. It will take good habits, proper attitudes, right thinking and correct actions. It will take establishing goals and working toward them with all your heart and resolve.

Look at the most successful people in the world and ask yourself, *what did they do that was different from everyone else?* The next important questions are: *Are you taking the path that those elite few chose; and are you doing the things necessary to bring you early success, or are you following the crowd of mediocrity?* I personally refuse to be a follower. I believe there are extraordinary successes in my future, but I know that I will have to work for them. I also know that I will not be able to follow the crowd in order to reach my goals. I will have to take the path less traveled, think outside the box, and focus my time and energy on achieving my dreams.

The world doesn't care whether you or I succeed or fail in life. It's up to you and me to care, and no one else. If you do care, however, then there are some things that you will need to do and put into practice, because you can't expect to achieve million-dollar dreams without effort. It has been said, *you can't expect something from nothing.* So we'll start with some key essential principles that have helped others reach their million-dollar dreams. I'll share those with you and tell you how I'm applying those principles to my life right now. Hopefully you'll see that if someone like me can do it, so can you.

Million-dollar dreams come in many forms, shapes, and sizes. Whether your dream is to have a million dollars by the age of 30, be a professional athlete, or any other dream that your heart leads you toward, this book will give you some guidance and insight on how to begin to achieve it. It doesn't matter what the dream is because as Gil Atkinson stated, *"You are one of a kind; therefore, no one can really predict to what heights you might soar. Even you will not know until you spread your wings!"* So let's start right now by taking that first step, spreading your wings, and discovering what great things you are capable of—all while working toward your million-dollar dreams.

Chapter 1

Million-Dollar Attitudes

"There is little difference in people,
but that little difference makes a big difference.
The little difference is attitude.
The big difference is whether it is positive or negative."
W. Clement Stone

I believe that attitude is one of the primary factors that determine whether or not you will achieve your million-dollar dreams—or any goal for that matter. The main reason for this is that without the proper attitude, you will never *have* million-dollar dreams in the first place. It takes the right attitude and belief in yourself to be able to dream big. You must be able to think big, believe that it can happen, break out of your comfort zone, and know that you have the inherent right to achieve your dreams as much as anyone else does. It's not as easy as it sounds, however. Many people get caught up in negative thinking or self-doubt and can't break free of it. When this happens, it holds them back from achieving their full potential. When it comes to million-dollar dreams, you cannot allow negativity or self-doubt to invade or replace your positive attitude and beliefs.

When asked, most people will say they are positive thinkers and maintain positive attitudes. That might be true in many areas; but is it true in all areas? The questions you have to ask yourself are: *Are you a positive thinker when it comes to money and success?* And, *do you have a positive attitude toward big thinkers with million-dollar dreams?* Often when people are introduced to those individuals who have money or success, or who are big thinkers with million-dollar dreams, the negative thoughts of *them* versus *us,* or the *haves* versus the *have nots* are immediately created. These are dangerous categories to believe in, because once you believe they exist, you must then place yourself in one area or the other. You immediately must become a *have* or a *have not,* and most likely, if you believe there is a difference, you will place yourself on the *have not* side of the fence. To better help you understand this I'll describe two people: Joe and Thomas – two young men *who looked through the same bars, but one saw mud and one saw stars.* [1]

Joe grew up in a middle-class home with both parents. His father worked at the local paper mill for over 30 years, and his mother worked as a teacher in the school system. Combined they had a little above-average income for the area, lived in a nice house and had most things they desired. Joe, however, hated the fact that there were others he grew up with who had more than he did. He put those people down whenever he had a chance, criticized them, and found excuses for their wealth or success. His statements were filled with *us* versus *them*, as if to say that they were a different breed of human very unlike him. He complained that if he had been born into a rich family, he too, would have had the things they had. When Joe graduated from high school, even though college was available to him, he chose to enter the work force at the local paper mill so that he could immediately buy the things he wanted in life.

Joe drew a line in the sand as a teen and stood on the *have-not* side. This line was not simply a line he could cross, because to him, it was the Grand Canyon. He believed the differences were so great between the *haves* and *have-nots*, that he limited his own potential based on those beliefs.

Thomas also grew up in the same small town, and his father also worked at the same local paper mill. His mother was a cleaning lady for some of the more wealthy people in town. Their combined income was below average for the area; they lived in a modest house, and often went without the newest shoes or toys in order to pay the bills. Thomas, however, had a different outlook than Joe. Yes, he saw that there were many others who had a lot more than he had, but he didn't seem to mind. He got to know the people who were richer or more successful than his family was. He found that these people were hard workers and made sacrifices just like his parents did. But he also found that they had goals and dreams they believed in, and an attitude that would help to make them a reality. They were confident, optimistic and excited about what they were doing, and most of all, they were eager and willing to help others reach their goals. When Thomas graduated, he continued on to college, and soon after began his own successful business.

Thomas never created self-limiting canyons to cross and never placed people in categories that excluded him. He believed there was very little difference between people, and knew that if others could dream big and achieve their goals, so could he. He believed, as William James stated, *"Human beings, by changing the inner attitudes of their minds, can change the outer aspects of their lives."* Thomas did not resign himself to the role in which he was born. He had greater ambitions and aspired to achieve them.

I'm not saying that simply by having a positive attitude you will become a millionaire or achieve your million-dollar dreams; but I *am* saying that it is a key ingredient. You need belief in your dreams and belief in yourself, as well as belief that you are deserving and worthy enough to achieve those dreams. For some reason, many people put limitations on their dreams because they don't believe they deserve to be rich or achieve success. Many don't even believe that they deserve happiness. But you have to believe this! No one deserves to live in poverty, failure or unhappiness. You do not have to live the life of your parents if they lived that way. You can create the life you want, but it all begins with envisioning the successes and happiness that you desire in your life. It all starts with visualizing the future you want to create. Walt Disney is a perfect example of this, and his comment, *"If you can dream it, you can do it,"* says it as simply as possible.

When I was in seventh grade I tried out for the junior high baseball team. I was one of two seventh graders who made the team, but was told that seventh graders wouldn't get any playing time. The eighth grade boys had been playing ball together since they were six years old and were all very talented ballplayers. They were the best players that our town had seen in a long while. I was faced with two choices: I could place these eighth grade players in the category of *haves* (players with more talent and more ability than I had) and myself in a *have-not* category, or I could choose to see them very similar to me with only minor differences. I knew I could work on those differences and with the right attitude and beliefs I could compete at their level. I chose the latter.

I didn't start in the first game, but as I sat on the bench I kept visualizing myself on the field making the plays, hitting and throwing the ball, and rounding the bases. I believed I could compete. Our second game of the season our pitcher didn't show up for the game and the coach asked who else could pitch. I raised my hand even though I was a shortstop. That game I pitched a no-hitter, hit two three-run triples and a grand slam. I started every game after that.

Then I entered high school and tried out for the varsity baseball team. I had to compete with sophomores, juniors and seniors. Again, these players could have become the *haves* and I the *have-not*, but I refused to think like that—even when my name wasn't on the initial varsity roster after tryouts. The coach then had us play a few pre-season games prior to choosing his final roster. I was given an opportunity to show him what I could do. I knew in my mind that I could succeed and make the team, and that's what I did. I believed in myself and in my goal of being a varsity player as a freshman. I played hard, made the team, and ended up the only freshman in the starting line-up. That year I received an award for defensive player of the year, and was the only freshman chosen for the All-Conference team. My coach, Richard Whitten, was quoted in the magazine *Business Focus,* as saying, *"It's very hard for a freshman to step in and play with an older team. Not only has Kris played exceptionally well. He actually carried the team for awhile. I have to say that he's exceeded excellent at this point in his career."*

I also played well my sophomore and junior year and realized that the next step for me would require a huge leap of faith and belief in myself. Before my senior year of high school I asked my parents if we could move from Maine to Florida so that I could play baseball year-round and compete with some of the best players in the country in order to see if I really had talent. My family ended up moving, and I entered my senior year of high school in a new state and new environment much different than the one I was accustomed to.

Once again I was told that I would never make the team, let alone get any playing time. I was going to be competing with players who had been playing year-round since they were five years old and had won many championships together. I only played a couple months a year, but I wasn't going to let my dreams die. I refused to get caught up in other people's negative thinking. Instead, I worked very, very hard, kept my positive attitude, and envisioned the results I wanted and proved them wrong. I made the starting line-up, and once again achieved my goals. I lead the conference in triples and scoring, and I made All-Conference. I didn't have the year I wanted to have, but due to my performance I received a scholarship to a top Division I college.

Without a positive attitude and right thinking I never would have believed I was deserving or good enough to have the goals that I did. I had to make sure that I didn't fall into the trap of creating a canyon between the other players and me. There were no *haves* or *have-nots* in my thinking, and if there *were*, I was going to be one of the *haves*. I had to think big, break out of my comfort zone, believe in myself, and visualize my goals. I never would have achieved them if I hadn't done this. But most of all, I never would have achieved any of it without the dream in the first place.

You can dream big at any age. You don't have to be 50 years old to have big goals. You can be 12 years old, 17 years old or 25. At all times and all ages you need to have dreams. Then by putting your million-dollar attitude to work, along with belief in yourself, acceptance of your worthiness, and visualization of the desired outcome, the possibility of achieving those dreams will begin to become a reality for you.

Million-Dollar Thoughts

Have you drawn any negative lines in the sand or created self-limiting canyons? If so, think back to when and why you created them. Then visualize a positive image in your mind that is the total opposite of your original thinking. Every time your thoughts wander back to your original negative thinking, say STOP, and replace the thought with your new positive thought.

Million-Dollar Affirmation

I deserve success and happiness and as a result am achieving my million-dollar dreams.

Million-Dollar Action

Describe what you would look like if you had already achieved your million-dollar dream. What would your home, your relationships and your life be like?

_____

_____

_____

_____

_____

_____

Read what you have written aloud and say, *I deserve this, and I can achieve it!*

Chapter 2

Million-Dollar Habits

"Good habits result from resisting temptation."
Albert Einstein

I remember when I was nine years old and in fourth grade and a few boys teased me because I was wearing a department store brand sneaker. They griped that they were poor and I was richer than they were and said that I should be wearing Nike sneakers, not a department store brand. Until then I never noticed any difference between anyone's sneakers nor the difference between who might be rich and who might be poor based on what they wore. I was confused because those boys who claimed to be poor were all wearing the sneakers they told me *I* should be wearing. I went home that day and asked my parents why I didn't have Nike sneakers. They told me that often people placed too much emphasis on status items such as clothing or cars. I would have to learn to make choices—to spend on the things that everyone else had, or to invest in something that might be much more important to me later on such as my dreams and my goals.

A nine year-old may have difficulty with this choice, but as I grew up I continued to hear stories from my parents that emphasized the point they were trying to make years before. Both of my parents worked in the financial industry and would often express their frustration when people with good incomes took no steps toward their professed goals. Many had goals of retiring early, taking annual family vacations, buying a new home or going back to school; but instead of investing toward these goals, they spent all their disposable income from their weekly paychecks on other items. These people indulged in their latest whims and bought expensive clothes, expensive toys, snowmobiles or 4-wheelers (as examples). Most of these purchases were impulse purchases because they wanted to keep up with the Joneses. They needed that shot of immediate gratification to make them feel better about themselves. But what they didn't recognize is that by doing this, they lost out on achieving their goals. But to make matters worse, these people complained and complained and took on the role of the victim and blamed their employers for their lack of money to meet their professed goals.

Alright, so maybe the *true* goals of these people were not as they stated, and their *true* goals were to have all of these material items. Whether that was the case or not, these stories helped create my mindset of investing in my goals and dreams versus spending to achieve some form of immediate satisfaction.

As I grew older I understood this more clearly. I could immediately have the $100 Nike sneakers *(that I would most likely grow out of in four months),* or I could save my money and get a new bat or glove or maybe even a pitching machine, which would all help further my baseball goals. When I looked at spending in this light, the answer was very clear to me.

I thought this was an easy concept to understand, but day after day I watched my friends spend every penny they made as soon as they made it. The more they made, the more they spent. I, on the other hand, kept saving and saving and only spent on those things that I felt were very important to achieving my goals. Yet I seemed to be in the minority.

The more I looked around, the more I saw everyone spending not saving. There seemed to be a powerful force of temptation pulling these people toward numerous ways to create distance between them and their money. I can't say that this habit of spending is a right or a wrong way of life for you as an individual, but if you have million-dollar dreams, this type of spending habit will not get you where you want to go. You will need to resist the temptation to spend and the temptation to achieve some sort of immediate satisfaction in order to gain achievement of your goals. I think I Ching states it best: *"The man who pursues pleasures and self-gratification will never achieve anything so long as he is surrounded by dissipating temptations."* This basically means that as long as you pursue temptations that have no lasting effect (such as inappropriate spending), you will not achieve your solid goals that could have lasting effects on your future.

Man has always had difficulty resisting temptation since Adam and Eve and the forbidden fruit. The temptation to spend is as powerful as any temptation anyone is faced with today. It is not easy to resist when you are bombarded with advertisements to spend every minute of your life. You are promised everything from health to beauty, from sex appeal to pleasure. Everyone wants you to spend, spend, and spend.

To make matters worse, now you have the ability to spend money *you don't even have* through the magic of credit cards. Offers for pre-approved credit cards mount in mailboxes, and most people do not have the willpower to just throw them away. Instead they are once again enticed to spend. Today credit card debt burdens 55,000,000 Americans, and the average person has $7,000 of non-essential debt. So you have a choice to make. You can become one of the 55,000,000, or one of the few that save and only spend on the things that will have lasting effects—those items that will bring you closer to your million-dollar dreams.

There are actually millions of reasons why people spend, but that is for a book on psychology of spending. The fact of the matter is that if you really want to achieve your million-dollar dreams, you need to curb your spending and start investing. To do this you first have to place a million-dollar value on yourself and on your dreams. Second you have to invest only in those things that bring you closer to realizing your dreams.

Think a moment about this statement made by Malcolm Forbes. *"Too many people overvalue what they are not and undervalue what they are."* It's easy to do this, but instead you need to do the reverse. You need to value what you *are*, not what you *are not*. You are *not* your neighbors; and therefore, do not have to have everything they have. You are *not* your car, your house, your toys or your job. You are *not* what you spend your money on. These items are *not* where your value comes from. Your true value comes from within. It's who you are and what you stand for. It's your drive and your purpose. It's YOU! Once you realize this, it's easy to only spend on those items that encourage and support you and your dreams!

Over the years I began to realize that ultimately I was the one responsible for my financial choices and financial situation. If I chose to spend foolishly, I would find that I didn't have the funds to meet my goals. If I saved and invested, I would. No amount of complaining or blame would change that. You need to realize that you are ultimately the only one responsible for your future. Without this knowledge you will think differently and create different habits. Those *without* million-dollar dreams create *poor-minded* spending habits and then make excuses for their lack or inability to achieve their professed goals. They play the role of victim and say, *poor me*. They blame their employer, the economy and the government. They complain and complain, but do nothing to change their habits.

My challenge to you is to start creating *rich-minded* habits. Prioritize your spending, and invest in yourself and your dreams first. I believe that if you do this, you will be one step closer to achieving your million-dollar dreams.

But there is more to your habits than simply spending money. There is the critical factor of time—how you spend it, and what you spend it on. Everyone is given the same amount of time each day. It doesn't matter whether you are rich or poor, smart or not so smart, successful or not so successful. You've all been given the same 24 hours. The only difference in those 24 hours is how you spend it.

The Time Bank
Author Unknown

Imagine there is a bank that credits your account each morning with $86,400. It carries over no balance from day to day. Every evening it deletes whatever part of the balance you failed to use during the day. What would you do? Draw out ALL OF IT, of course!

Each of us has such a bank. Its name is TIME. Every morning it credits you with 86,400 seconds. Every night it writes off, as lost, whatever of this you have failed to invest to good purpose. It carries over no balance. It allows no overdraft.

Each day it opens a new account for you. Each night it burns the remains of the day. If you fail to use the day's deposits, the loss is yours. There is no going back and living off the past. There is no drawing against tomorrow.

You must live in the present on today's deposits. Invest it as to get from it the utmost in health, happiness, and success! The clock is running. Make the most of today.[2]

I'm uncertain who the author of *The Time Bank* is, but it is perfect for discussing time. Everyone has the same 365 days, 8,760 hours per year. Most people work an average of 8-hours per working day or 1,944 hours per year. They sleep an average of 2,920 hours, leaving them with 3,896 hours per year (which is approximately 8-10 hours per day!). **What are they spending *all* these hours doing?** Research shows that the average adult spends 4 ½ hours per day watching TV. That's over 1,642 hours a year! When you start looking at time this way, you will begin to think differently and become more aware of how you might be wasting it.

Think for a moment about how you spend your time. On weekends, summer break or vacations, how late do you sleep? Do you sit in front of the TV all day? Do you party with your friends all night?

How many books do you read a year? Do you read the newspaper? Are you current on world events? Do you study your area of business to know the most and be the best?

How much time do you spend on reaching your goals? How much effort do you put into making your dreams come true? Do you take the actions necessary to make them happen, or only dream about them? Are you focused on what really counts?

The Bible says, what you sow you will reap. If you sow good habits, you will reap the rewards. When you pay your bills on time, you reap good credit. When you read, you learn something new and reap additional knowledge. When you set a goal, you reap the ability to achieve it.

If you really want to achieve your dreams, you will have to spend the time necessary to accomplish them. Without this concerted effort, it will not happen.

Many of my teammates spent a lot of time playing video games and watching TV. I preferred to be outside swinging my bat with my Solo-Hitter. *(A Solo-Hitter is a baseball-training device to allow you to swing your bat and hit a baseball over and over.)* I would beg my father to pitch balls to me or to play long toss. I spent hours and hours practicing and would swing the bat 400 times a day.

On evenings and weekends, a lot of the people I knew would go to parties. This was fine and often fun, but many ended up drinking or doing drugs at them as well. I didn't choose this path because I wanted to keep my body as healthy as possible. Did I lose my friends because I didn't drink or do drugs? No. My friends respected me and my decisions and choices. Good friends always will. If they don't, then they aren't good friends to begin with.

I wasn't willing to succumb to peer pressure because I knew it would get in the way of my dreams. Some might think that one night of drinking would not do that. But to me when you allow yourself to compromise your values or your time even once, I believe it can easily lead to future compromises.

Hopefully everyone reading this book will have seen the 1976 movie, *Rocky*. Rocky was an underdog boxer who got a chance to fight Apollo Creed for the world heavyweight boxing title. Even though the fight was originally planned as a publicity stunt by Apollo Creed, it became a chance for Rocky to prove himself as a prizefighter. It was a huge stretch for Rocky to even believe he was good enough to stand in the same ring with someone like Apollo, but this was his dream—his million-dollar dream. Did he see Apollo as a *have* and himself as a *have-not?* No. He saw himself as a champion, but he also knew that he wouldn't be this champion without good habits of dedication, determination and hard work. He knew that every waking hour of his life needed to be dedicated to working toward his dream.

So did Rocky stay up late, party, eat the wrong foods, sit in front of the TV or sleep the day away? Of course not. He got his sleep, ate right *(remember those gross protein egg drinks he drank),* got up early and trained hard. He did the things necessary for him to accomplish his dream. Yes he struggled. Yes it was hard. But he overcame the odds because he made himself and his dream a priority. He believed in his dream and created the habits that would support it. He worked hard to become the best, and fought for his dream with all of his strength, heart and soul.

Rocky had a burning desire to achieve his dream, and he did what it took to accomplish it. Marsha Sinetar says, *"Burning desire to be or do something gives us staying power."* We need that burning desire inside of us—

our million-dollar dreams. And we need to create the habits that nourish them. Mastering your habits is choosing to live your life with your eyes open—being aware of what you are doing at all times and why you are doing it.

So the question is: *how bad do you want to achieve your dreams?* And, *are you willing to maintain the habits that will make them a reality?* For someone with million-dollar dreams, the answer has to be yes. But more than a *yes* answer, there has to be action associated with it.

Million-Dollar Thoughts

Think back over the past month. What did you spend your money on? Did you save or invest any funds for future use toward your million-dollar dreams? How did you spend your free time? If the answers to these questions do not coincide with the necessary answers to achieve your million-dollar dreams, then you will need to create better habits. Scrutinize all related actions over the next month and change the negative habits into positive habits.

Million-Dollar Affirmation

I invest my money and my time wisely in ways that reinforce the achievement of my million-dollar dreams.

Million-Dollar Action

After each word below, list a positive action that you can take that will help bring you closer to your million-dollar dreams.

Spending: _____

_____

Investing: _____

_____

Time: _____

_____

Chapter 3

Million-Dollar Mentality

"If you want to succeed, you should strike out on new paths rather than travel the worn paths of accepted success."
John D. Rockefeller, Jr.

According to actuarial tables, if you take 100 people now age 25 and check in on them when they are 65, you will find that only five of the 100 end up financially independent. Fifteen would have modest savings, and 80 would be totally broke!

According to the U.S. Census Bureau, in 2003, those people earning $127,904 per year were in the top 5% of earners in America. The medium income (or middle-class) was approximately $42,409, and the bottom 50% of Americans earned $28,528 or less.

Consider this as well. The average net worth of the top 1% was $10,204,000. For the middle-class it was $40,200. The average net worth of the bottom 50% of earners was $1,900, yet 50% of workers in this category had no savings at all.

What creates such huge differences between the top 1% to 5% of earners and the middle class and bottom 50% of wage earners? Many factors do, including attitude and habits, but I also believe there is another vital difference— the difference between having an *employee mentality* or an *entrepreneur mentality*.

The largest percent of individuals in America have an employee mentality. These people consider no other options other than that they will get a job and work for someone else. They believe that this is where they will find the most job security and most opportunity. Yes, they want *good* jobs with *good* income, but regardless, they plan on working for someone else forever.

Most people I know have this mentality. I recently took a business class at a local college, and the professor asked the students how many were planning on being an entrepreneur and building their own business, and how many were planning on working for others. Needless to say, I was the only person that had *no* intention of being an employee.

The ironic part of the employee mentality is that these individuals believe that being an employee for someone else creates the most job security. They see this as the less-risky form of work. Unfortunately jobs today have become less stable and less available. Businesses close daily leaving thousands upon thousands unemployed.

In the small town where I grew up there were three major employers that employed a large number of the town and surrounding town's population. The individuals who worked there enjoyed nice weekly paychecks for years. Then, the unthinkable happened. Within just a few short years of each other, two of the three employers closed their doors forever, and an overseas company bought out the third. The changes with these three companies left thousands of workers unemployed. The town and employees were in shock because they had felt by working for one of these companies that they had life-long job security. No one saw this coming, and all of a sudden there were thousands of people scrambling for other jobs – jobs where there were 100s of applicants for each position.

While this won't happen to everyone who holds a job, it is happening to many. Businesses are closing, moving overseas or are outsourcing their jobs. I understand that not everyone can work for himself, and there will always be the need for employees, but I believe that there is more job security in maintaining and living with an *entrepreneur mentality* than depending on a company to support you.

What is an entrepreneurial mentality?

- ◆ It is a mentality that makes *you* responsible for your career and opportunities.

- ◆ It is a mentality that does not limit you to one employer or one job.

◆ It is a mentality that helps you to create your own sources of income.

◆ It is a mentality that is flexible and can change easily based on the economy, your situation, or the needs of others.

◆ It is a mentality that helps you seek out multiple sources of income instead of having your income come from only one source.

◆ And it is a mentality that looks for residual income, which means that when you stop working, your money doesn't, and it keeps working and keeps coming in.

I'm going to share with you a little about three different millionaires who practice the art of the entrepreneur mentality.

Michael Dell, who created Dell computer, has been a true entrepreneur since the second grade when he started his first business selling candy. A few years later he created a direct-mail business selling stamps. In high school he bought a computer, studied it and began upgrading old computers and reselling them to his friends for a profit. While continuing to upgrade and sell computers in high school and college, he took a job selling newspaper subscriptions. While this wasn't a very profitable business at first, Dell took one step farther and researched who bought subscriptions and who didn't. He found that those that took a new subscription to the paper were those who had just moved or were recently married. Dell began gathering the names of everyone who had recently applied for a marriage license, contacted them and sales skyrocketed. He then took all of the commissions he made from the paper and invested it in more computers. He could have bought expensive cars and toys, but instead chose to invest in his million-dollar dreams. Soon he was making over $80,000 a year from his computer business and decided that if he did this full time he would make millions—which he did.

Cory Rudl, Internet marketing guru, did not put all of his eggs into one basket and understood the true meaning of multiple sources of income. He developed a system to generate income from numerous products and sources, and then automated those streams of income so he could move to his next idea. The goal was to create several streams of income from many different sources so that if one idea failed, he wouldn't have to worry because the other sources continued to make money every month. He was successful in this concept and now generates over $7 million-dollars a year in sales.

At the age of 23, Nancy Collins knew that corporate America was not what she wanted to rely on for her future. Her father worked at the same company for 50 years and then was tossed away like an old shoe at age 68. He had nothing to show for his years of hard work. Nancy refused to let that happen to her so she decided to take her earning ability into her own hands. She quit her job as an administrative assistant and started earning commissions based on her own actions in a network marketing company. She made $60,000 her first year, and by the time she was 30 had made over a million dollars.

I also always wanted to be an entrepreneur, even though I didn't know what the word meant in the beginning. It all began at the early age of three or four when I began collecting things. I collected coins, rocks, PVC figurines and anything else that caught my interest. By the time I reached the age of eight my interest had turned to baseball cards. I soon found myself negotiating for the purchase or sale of these cards with friends and even card dealers. By the age of 12 I discovered the Internet and realized I could reach a lot more card collectors besides those in my own hometown. My business took off, and not only was I selling and buying, I was brokering deals for other people. Many people on the Internet considered me an expert in the area of up-and-coming prospects. Little did they know that I was under the age of 15.

In high school I was making excellent money and had set a goal for myself to make enough money to pay for my college education. I began re-investing my profits either in more card inventory or the stock market. At the age of 16 I invested in my first stock and within a few months I had made a $60,000 profit on it. Unfortunately later the stock tumbled and so did my profit, but it taught me about timing and being more aware of a right time to buy and sell. In the meantime, many of my friends saw how successful my business was going and wanted to do what I was doing; but they didn't want to put in the work, the research, or spend the time it took. They wanted me to do it for them. When I tried to teach them, they weren't committed enough to do it and chose to mow lawns or scoop ice cream instead.

I knew from a young age that I wanted to be responsible for my own career. I wanted to be in a business where *I* had control over my income and my future net worth instead of allowing someone else to determine what my work was worth. Even though my dream was to become a professional baseball player, I also realized the importance of having a plan B and creating other sources of income. I maintained a flexible mentality that allowed me to change with the times and circumstances. Finally, I also looked for means of residual income. I made sure that my money was invested so that it was working for me, even when I wasn't.

I'm certain that no one chooses to be in the bottom 50% of Americans who have little-to-no net worth and minimal incomes. However, many do find themselves content to be in the middle-class sector. There is nothing wrong with this, but if you have million-dollar dreams, you need to acquire an entrepreneur mentality, break free of your comfort zone, and start working toward results.

When you look again at the net-worth differences between the top 1% of the population *($10,204,000)* and bottom 50% *($1,900)*, it might scare you away from even attempting to reach your million-dollar financial dreams. The difference is astronomical. But there isn't such a huge difference between medium (middle-class) incomes *($42,409)* versus the top 5% of earners in America *($127,904)*.

Many entrepreneurs simply look at this as a numbers game. If they can double their money each year, they will reach their financial goals. Let's say you start out with $5,000. $5,000 doubled every year for eight years will give you over $1,000,000. Once you have your $1,000,000, if you continue to double it each year, you will be in the top 1% of the population in a little less than 4 years.

Obviously not everyone can double their money every year, but that's the challenging part. Achieving any million-dollar dream will be full of hard work and exciting challenges. That's what makes it fun. If it's *not* fun, then you need to re-evaluate your goals, because this should be an enjoyable, challenging, and fun process for you. The goal isn't simply to reach the end result. The goal should be to enjoy the process of *trying* to reach it. Like so many successful people have said before, *"Success is a journey, not a destination."*

I may never reach my goal of becoming a professional baseball player or being in the top financial 1% of the population, but so far, the process has been really fun. Having an entrepreneurial mentality challenges me. It forces me to stretch and work harder than I might otherwise. In that also comes a sense of satisfaction, knowing that I am taking the steps forward toward my dreams.

Million-Dollar Thoughts

Every million-dollar dream is like a new business, and you are the entrepreneur starting it. What can you do to start acting like the owner and boss of your company instead of an employee? How do you need to change your thinking?

Million-Dollar Affirmation

I am an entrepreneur—the owner of my million-dollar dream. I am responsible for making my dream fun, rewarding, and successful.

Million-Dollar Action

If you hired someone to be the president of your company (the person that would lead your company to the successful achievement of your million-dollar dreams), what would that individual's resume look like? How would you expect them to act and think?

_____

_____

_____

_____

How do you compare to this person? Do you need to improve your resume so that you are the most qualified individual to lead your company to success? Examine your weaknesses and strengths and improve both.

Chapter 4

Million-Dollar Thinking

"I like thinking big. If you're going to be thinking anything, you might as well think big."
Donald Trump

What do the following people all have in common? Sir Isaac Newton, Christopher Columbus, Albert Einstein, Aristotle, Martin Luther King, Orville and Wilbur Wright, Napoleon Bonaparte, Thomas Edison, Adolf Hitler, Plato, Alexander Graham Bell, Ludwig van Beethoven, Michelangelo, Thomas Jefferson, Joseph Stalin, Julius Caesar, Sigmund Freud, John F. Kennedy, Henry Ford and Jesus Christ.

The answer is simple. They were all million-dollar thinkers. Because of their limitless ability to think beyond the scope of history and their current environment, our world changed dramatically. Even though we may not have agreed with some of their thinking and resultant actions, there is no doubt that these people were still million-dollar thinkers. Keep in mind that by calling them million-dollar thinkers does not mean that they all had goals of becoming millionaires. (Albert Einstein for example never amassed any wealth.) It simply means that they all had ideas and goals of great importance to them that they were willing to pursue.

Unfortunately, some of these people, like Adolf Hitler and Joseph Stalin, used their big-thinking ability to harm, not help. It is obviously my wish that all of you use your big thinking to change the lives around you in a positive way. In my opinion, million-dollar thinking should create success, achievement and happiness. I believe, as Buckminster Fuller did, *"The purpose of our lives is to add value to the people of this generation and those that follow."* Because of this, it is my hope that you use your million-dollar thinking for good, not evil, and remember that million-dollar thinking is not just about you. It's about living true to your purpose and sharing your gifts with as many people as possible.

What is your biggest dream? What would you do if you knew you could be successful at anything? These are important questions to ask yourself because you have to *have* a dream in order for it to become a reality. You need to know what you want from life because it is ultimately up to you to create it. There aren't many people who can state exactly what their dreams are for their entire lives because dreams are always changing. However, at each stage in your life, you should have a dream for that moment. Without one, your life flounders without direction. And if your dreams and goals are limited, you'll get limited results.

I, of course, look at my dreams and goals in terms of baseball. The question I ask myself is, *do I want to play in the big league or the little league?* For me that's easy, and it should be for you as well. If I am going to have dreams and goals, they might as well be big and abundant versus small.

Once you decide to think big and have million-dollar dreams, however, many people will try to derail you and hold you back from achieving them. Think about Christopher Columbus and his goal of finding a westward passage to the Indies. How many people tried to stop him from sailing in the direction of his dreams? Due to their limited thinking they believed the earth was flat and that he would fall off the edge of the world.

Thomas Edison is another example. He believed he could produce light. People laughed at him and thought he was crazy during his thousands of unsuccessful attempts to do this. He could have easily given up on his dreams due to the pressure he was faced with, but, thankfully, did not.

Big thinkers are often faced with other people's small thinking. Mark Twain gives the advice to, *"Keep away from people who try to belittle your ambitions."* Instead, persevere and the results will be rewarding; and even if you don't reach the stars as you had planned, you will most likely reach the moon.

So how do you begin to think big? First, figure out what you are really passionate about and really want to accomplish. Shut your eyes and let your imagination run wild. Once you can begin to visualize your dream, set a few goals that will help to achieve it. Then stop and think BIGGER to unlock your unlimited potential and set your *million-dollar goals*. These million-dollar goals should stir your blood and get you excited about taking action.

The second step is to write your goals down. While you might not think this is very important, it is critical. In 1953 Yale University conducted a study of its graduates that compared the success of those who wrote their goals down to those who didn't. Twenty years later in 1973, the 3% of the class who had comprehensive written goals had accomplished more than all of the other 97% combined! This one test alone should tell you something.

Now that you have a clear idea of your goals and have written them down, begin to really *feel* them. Picture yourself accomplishing them. Envision exactly what it will look and feel like once you achieve your desired results. David J. Schwartz, author of *The Magic Of Thinking BIG* states, *"Nothing happens, no forward steps are taken until a goal is established."* Setting your goals and knowing what you want has to be the first step. The second step is to write them down. The third step is to visualize them.

When you internalize your million-dollar dreams and the goals it will take to accomplish them, you'll become so confident, determined and persistent that you will be able to achieve all that you set your mind to. Motivational speaker, Anthony Robbins states, *"Most people have no idea of the giant capacity we can immediately command when we focus all of our resources on mastering a single area of our lives."*

At this point, it is time to put your mind to work to achieve your dreams by controlling your thoughts and attitudes. Tom Blandi states, *"Our attitudes control our lives. Attitudes are a secret power working 24 hours a day, for good or bad. It is of paramount importance that we know how to harness and control this great force."*

Norman Vincent Peale made positive thinking famous through his book, *The Power Of Positive Thinking.* His book was originally published in 1952. It was later translated into 42 languages and has since sold over 20 million copies! Dr. Peale's belief is simple, *that we get what we expect.* If we expect success, we get it. If we expect failure, we get that too. How much simpler could that be?

It is also believed that our thoughts are magnetic. Positive thoughts attract positive results—just like a magnet. But in the same breath, negative thoughts attract negative results. Basically, your brain cannot determine what you truly want. It is simply attracting what you are focusing on and thinking about. So when you establish your million-dollar dreams, make sure you focus on achieving them in a positive manner because you will be setting in motion the law of attraction. This magnetic force will find a way of attracting and accomplishing exactly what you are thinking about.

Some people call this the law of attraction, while others call it manifestation. It is believed that your entire life, conditions, relationships and outcomes are the product of your thinking. Dr. Wayne Dyer is a master when it comes to teaching manifestation. He introduced the world to ancient Eastern, private spiritual and mystical principles that have been around before the Judeo/Christian culture itself. Practiced, it is believed that you can literally attract what you want, thereby, manifesting the destiny that you want.

In simpler terms, thinking *does* make it so, because how you think determines how you act, and how you act determines whether or not you will achieve your goals. Your thinking is critical to your success.

You may be saying to yourself that all of this is a little *out there* for you, so for those who want scientific data, that, too, is available. What scientists have learned about the human brain in the past six years is blowing them away. They now know that humans think on six different levels at once, yet only 1/6th of it is at a conscious level. The remaining 5/6th is on a sub-conscious level, meaning that your sub-conscious is controlling most of your thoughts, and acting automatically 83% of the time.

Doug Bench, a leading expert in neuroscience research, explains that every action you take in your life is preceded by a thought impulse. Therefore, your total phys-ical world today reflects all of the thinking you have (or have not) been doing throughout your life. You have in your life today exactly what you have been telling yourself you want in your life. This can be bad news for you if you don't currently have in your life what you want, but the good news is that your sub-conscious brain cells detect and pick up information up to 800 times faster than your conscious brain cells. Because of this, you have the ability to control your thoughts every second of every day. You have the ability to re-train your brain if you want to achieve more. This is the greatest wonder of neuroscience.

Doug Bench states, *"If you change the quality of your thinking, you will change the quality of your life. When you change and take full responsibility for how you think about yourself, your relationships, your goals, your achievements and your world, your life will change too!"*[3]

When you begin to re-train the 83% sub-conscious part of your brain with positive, re-affirming thought impulses that encourage success, there will be no limit to what you can do. But I like how Napoleon Hill, author of *Think & Grow Rich,* says it, *"Whatever the mind can conceive, and believe, it can achieve"* and will.

For those of you with a religious background, this same concept applies, but instead of in a scientific form, in a spiritual form. In the Bible it states, *"Ask and you shall receive."* (John 16). *"If you believe, you will receive whatever you ask for in prayer."* (Matthew 21). *"Whatever you ask for in prayer, believe that you have received it, and it will be yours."* (Mark 11) God continually tells you how to achieve what you desire – by asking and believing.

So whether you want to believe God's word, scientific research, ancient manifestation, the law of attraction, or the power of positive thinking, it doesn't really matter, because all of them will give you the same results. The results will be based on your thinking.

Michael Leuboeuf remarked, *"The world is your mirror and your mind is a magnet. What you perceive in this world is largely a reflection of your own attitudes and beliefs. Life will give you what you attract with your thoughts. Think, act and talk negatively and your world will be negative. Think and act and talk with enthusiasm and you will attract positive results."*

When you really begin to think about this, I am certain that you will come up with numerous examples of how this has worked in your life. For me, if I had gone to the plate thinking that I would never hit the ball and strike out, I'm sure that would have been the result. I can't imagine any other result other than striking out if that's what I believed I would do, because I would be telling my subconscious to do just that. On the other hand, I recall a time when I was a freshman and our team faced one of the best pitchers in the State. He had a 90+ mile-per-hour fast-ball that no one could hit. My teammates were striking out left and right. I convinced myself that I could, and would, get a hit off this guy. I visualized myself watching the ball and hitting it at just the right time. When it was my turn at bat, everything I had played previously in my mind took over and I hit the ball – right out of the ballpark! I was the only player in the entire season to hit a home run off this pitcher, and I was only a puny freshman. I believe it had everything to do with my thoughts (and maybe a little bit of talent). While all the other players had convinced themselves that no one could get a hit off this guy, I was telling myself that I could. Each of us got exactly what we convinced ourselves we would get. This one event led me to believe that I might really have the potential and the mindset to achieve any million-dollar dream I might conceive.

Personally, I believe thoughts are very powerful, and I am focused on keeping them positive. It certainly can't hurt. When thinking about your million-dollar dreams, be careful how and what you think about them. Keep your thoughts focused on exactly what you want to achieve, and reap the rewards of your positive thinking.

Million-Dollar Thoughts

If changing the quality of your thinking can help you succeed in achieving your million-dollar dreams, wouldn't you do it? You have nothing to lose and everything to gain, so give it a try. Each night before falling asleep and each morning before rising, spend a moment thinking about what you want, and think about achieving it. Throughout the day focus on positive thoughts associated with it. Do this for 30 days or until it becomes a habit and reap the rewards.

Million-Dollar Affirmation

I think BIG. I think Positive; and I dream
Million-Dollar Dreams.

Million-Dollar Action

What are you passionate about achieving?

_____

Write down a goal associated with this.

_____

Think bigger. If you could not fail, what would the goal now be? _____

Think BIGGER, and write down a million-dollar dream.

_____

Chapter 5

Million-Dollar Drive

*"Desire is the key to motivation, but it's the
determination and commitment to an unrelenting
pursuit of your goal – a commitment to excellence – that
will enable you to attain the success you seek."*
Mario Andretti

In third grade I was given my first I.Q. test along
with our state's achievement tests. When our scores were
available, they were given to us in sealed envelopes with
strict instructions not to open them. They were only to be
opened by our parents. There were also strict instructions
not to compare these results or numbers with anyone—not
even with our friends. I carried that envelope, with my
name written neatly across the front, so carefully, as if it
was a ticking bomb and any quick movement would set it
off. All I knew was that the results in that envelope could
conceivable label me forever. My friends whispered back
and forth. One said it determined whether a kid was
mentally retarded or not. Fear and anxiety swept over us all.

When I got home I immediately gave my mother the envelope. I stood there as she opened it. She studied it for a long time, and then turned to me and said, *"Great job,"* and gave me a hug. She didn't look devastated, and she wasn't crying, so I must have done okay. I asked her if I could see it, and she let me see the achievement scores, but kept her finger carefully placed over the I.Q. testing score. I asked if I could see that number, but she refused, stating she didn't believe that any number could determine what a person was capable of and that it was meaningless.

Most people know the term I.Q., but what it really stands for is General Intelligence Quotient Score. It is a statistically derived number that indicates relative and comparative abilities that can be used to obtain academic skills and knowledge. *Boy that's a mouthful.* A person has hundreds of mental abilities, however, and the I.Q. test simply measures a couple of them; yet for some reason, people place a lot of importance on I.Q. testing.

Well, to this date my mother still hasn't told me what that number was. She knows it, but still won't share it, and that's okay. It might really bother me except for what I have been taught over the years by my parents. They have taught me that what a person achieves in life has nothing to do with his or her I.Q. A high I.Q. does not guarantee success or happiness; nor does a low I.Q. mean that an individual will be unsuccessful or unhappy. History is filled with stories of people with limited intellectual ability who have achieved greatness and been some of mankind's most important contributors. On the other hand, there are tales of woe, depression, isolation and even suicide for many considered geniuses.

I'm actually glad that my mother didn't share that number with me years ago. What if she had said, *"Your number is 100, which is a little below average."* Or, *"Your number is just average."* What do you think she would have set into motion? She would have set into motion my self-belief that I was just average, or below average in intellect. Therefore, I would have turned this knowledge into my reality. If I put belief into this number, *(and how could the experts who gave me this number be wrong,)* I would have lived my life at this level. I wouldn't have worked as hard or attempted things that I believed someone of this intellect would normally attempt.

Instead, my parents taught me that it was all about inner drive, ambition, desire and determination. A study of Harvard University graduates concurred. It found that 85% of everything a person achieves after college was the result of these traits, versus only 15% was a result of aptitude and abilities.[4]

Your ability to achieve your million-dollar dreams obviously doesn't only have to do with I.Q. and brainpower. Physical characteristics can also play a major role. Many limit themselves and their goals due to their own personal limiting beliefs about their physical characteristics. Society also tries to place limitations on people in many cases. Often it is thought that these limiting physical characteristics will completely deny you from achieving your goals, but history says that is not the case at all. If you have million-dollar dreams, but have characteristics that you, or others feel might limit your achievement of them, think again. You just need to ask yourself, how bad do you want to reach those goals, and can these physical characteristics be overcome or ignored completely? Your inner drive, ambition and desire will be deciding factors as to whether you succeed or not. Let me share with you a few examples of what I mean.

When society looks for a President of the United States, they probably imagine a statuesque, strong male. I think there are very few people who would imagine a man with polio sitting in a wheelchair. Yet did this stop Franklin D. Roosevelt from pursuing his million-dollar dream of becoming President of the United States? This man had to battle his physical affliction, but instead of using it as a crutch, he used it as a staff and compared it to the crippling effects of the Great Depression and won over the hearts of America. Thankfully, FDR set his goals and had the drive and ambition to achieve them and did not let any physical characteristic get in the way.

How about Helen Keller? Her remarkable story is known throughout the world. At the young age of 18 months, she contracted an illness that left her unable to see or hear. In the 1880s living a life of meaning and productivity with a disability such as this was unheard of. Most with disabilities were institutionalized forever because there was such great ignorance surrounding disabilities, along with limited medical and educational help for them. Helen Keller was faced with overwhelming odds, yet with determination and desire, as well as with the help of Anne Sullivan, Helen learned to read, write and speak. In 1904 Helen Keller was able to live a life that few others with disabilities such as hers lived. She graduated from Radcliffe College and later became a spokeswoman for the betterment of others. She did not allow this physical characteristic to stop her from achieving what she believed she was put on this earth to achieve. In fact, without this physical disability, she may never have had the impact that she did on so many lives.

Today I can think of one young man who is considered to be the epitome of drive, ambition, and desire, and that person is Tiger Woods. Is he a genius, or does he have a below average I.Q.? Who knows, and who cares? Is he the perfect physical specimen of a great golfer? Maybe. But did he have the colored skin of all great golfers before him? Definitely not. But do you think he used that as a self-limiting excuse as to why he *couldn't* achieve his dream of becoming the most famous golfer in the world? Absolutely not! Tiger Woods did not allow himself any excuses. He didn't care whether he was black, white or purple. His goal was to be the best, and that's what he set out to do. Many thought that he wouldn't be able to break the barriers of the past, but he didn't buy into that self-limiting thought. He allowed his desire to take over, pursued it with ambition, and used his drive and determination to accomplish it. Today he is the most famous golfer in the world as a result of it.

You may not have the highest I.Q. You may not be the strongest, the fastest, or the best. You may have a physical characteristic that is not common to others who have had similar goals in the past as you do; but none of this can stop you from achieving what you desire to achieve. Anatole France stated, *"Some succeed because they are destined to; most succeed because they are determined to."*

I've told you a bit about my baseball career, but what I haven't told you was that I was always one of the smallest guys on the team in high school. I stood 5'8" and weighed 160 pounds. I was competing with 6' tall, 200-pound athletes all the time. Think about this for a second. Who do you think could hit a baseball harder and faster? Someone like me, or someone much bigger? Your calculated guess probably isn't right. It had nothing to do with my I.Q. or size, but the fact that my desire to hit it harder than everyone else made me work at developing the skills I needed to do it. I developed my bat speed to the point where it compensated for my lack of size. Because I was so determined, I made it happen through hard work, preparation and desire.

Another person who also decided that nothing was going to stop him was Daniel "Rudy" Ruettiger. Rudy's father and older brother both worked in the local steel mill and never conceived any million-dollar dreams for themselves. Rudy, however, did. His dream was to attend Notre Dame to play football for the Fighting Irish. He had a poor academic record, mediocre athletic skills, and everyone told him it was impossible. *"My whole life people were telling me what I could do and what I couldn't do. I'd always listened to them, and I just didn't want to do that anymore. I had my own dream and there wasn't anything that was going to stop me from achieving it,"* Rudy said. For three semesters Rudy sought admission to Notre Dame as a transfer student, but each time he was rejected. He discovered that he had a mild case of dyslexia, learned to compensate for the condition and began to earn better grades, and finally was accepted into the University. His next step in achieving his dream was to make the football team, but at 5'6" and 165 pounds, again everyone told him it would never happen. Against all odds, however, he won a spot as a practice player on the scout team, which the varsity team ran its plays against. He was never allowed to suit up for games, but he *was* part of the team. While he had accomplished more than anyone ever believed he would, he still had the goal of playing in a *real* game. Over the next two years Rudy never missed a practice, and won the respect of his teammates, his coaches and the Notre Dame student body. At the final home game of the season, and the final game before Rudy graduated, Rudy was allowed to suit up and stand on the sidelines with the varsity players. He was finally able to be part of a *real* game. But something unexpected happened in the final moments of that game when the crowd began to chant, *"Ru-dy – Ru-dy – Ru-dy"*. With 27 seconds left on the clock Rudy's coach put him in the game; and in those seconds Rudy made his one and only tackle of his football career and sacked the quarterback. When the game ended, Rudy's teammates placed him upon their shoulders and carried him off the field. No player had ever been carried off the field like that before. Rudy achieved his million-dollar dream.

It took years of inner drive, ambition, desire and fierce determination for Rudy to achieve the dream he set for himself. It wasn't easy, but he never gave up. To this day, Rudy preaches what he practiced. He has built a career as a motivational speaker encouraging others to reach for the stars like he did.

Your inner drive and desire, ambition and determination are what push you forward when everyone and everything else is telling you to give up. It's what urges you to continue when moments of weakness and doubt enter your thoughts. It's what inspires you to forge ahead against all odds. Never give up on your dreams. Allow yourself to achieve them by reaching deep inside and harnessing these million-dollar characteristics.

Million-Dollar Thoughts

How bad do you want to achieve your million-dollar dreams? Who pushes you toward your dreams more than anyone? I hope the answer is: *I push myself forward more than anyone else.* If this is the case, it shows that you probably have what it takes *inside* to succeed. If this isn't your answer, stop and ask yourself why not?

Million-Dollar Affirmation

I have the inner drive, ambition, desire and determination to accomplish my million-dollar dreams.

Million-Dollar Action

Imagine a teenage girl wanting to go to her favorite singer's concert. She wants to attend so badly that she is willing to do extra chores around the house, babysit her little brother, give up her allowance, and even allow her mother to attend with her to chaperone—all the while being nice to everyone in the family the whole time! It doesn't matter what it will take. She is determined to do anything to go.

Recall a time when you felt this strongly about something. Remember that feeling. Then transfer that same feeling to your million-dollar dreams. Become so passionate about your dreams that your inner drive and desire will not allow you to give up. Develop so much desire and determination that you will be unable to fail, and then pursue your dreams with all your heart and resolve.

Chapter 6

Million-Dollar Opportunities

"In the middle of difficulty lies opportunity."
Sir Winston Churchill

At one time or another an unexpected event may change your ability to achieve your desired goal as originally planned. This could do one of four things:

1) It may force you to take a different direction or work harder in order to reach the same goal.

2) It may force you to make changes to your goal so that it is similar, but not exactly as you had originally planned, or

3) It may make you completely re-evaluate your goal, and take on a new goal.

4) It may make you give up entirely. (This, however, is *not* an option for anyone with million-dollar dreams.)

Having to seek a different direction, change a goal or re-evaluate a goal may make you feel as if you have failed. In my opinion, however, the word failure is extremely abused. The word failure simply means that you were either unsuccessful in your attempts, you met with adversity, or that you chose the wrong path. People fail all the time – all day long – each minute of the day, but people with million-dollar dreams don't give up after they have failed. This is why giving up entirely is not an option.

These unexpected events, setbacks, or failures simply give you an opportunity to grow and to move toward something better! Think again about Thomas Edison. Do you think the eleven thousand unsuccessful attempts prior to the invention of the light bulb would be considered failures or steps that brought him to success? Thomas Edison said, *"I have not failed. I have successfully discovered 1,200 materials that won't work."* People with million-dollar dreams never look at these setbacks in a negative light or consider them failures, but instead consider them unforeseen opportunities and steps that lead them closer to their dreams.

Unfortunately when you are faced with roadblocks to your dreams, most people don't immediately jump in and re-evaluate and see the opportunity in front of them. Instead they go through a grieving process that may include self-pity, blame, anger, and possibly even depression.

When you are faced with a major setback to your dreams, your first self-defensive reaction may be to see yourself as a victim of circumstances. This helps make the setback more palatable. Self-pity has become a very common reaction to painful circumstances and can become addictive because it numbs pain. It's not that self-pity makes you feel good, but it stops you from feeling bad. Self-pity can be very dangerous and destructive because it does not allow you to deal with your current situation in a constructive manner.

When you have finished with your pity party, you are faced with looking at your situation a little more closely. Still, you are not ready to look at it in a completely honest way, and it is easier to blame someone else for your setback. If it were someone else's fault, then it would have been beyond your control.

After you have convinced yourself that someone else is to blame, you actually become angry! You become angry with them, the situation, and even yourself. Take heart though. While this can be a very destructive stage, it actually means that you are moving forward. You wouldn't be human if you didn't experience some anger after a major setback in your life. Expressing this anger may be the only way you can go forward. The key is to not let the anger control you or get out of control. Don't hang on to it for too long because you need to let it go in order to move forward.

For those who hold on too long, depression may set in. If this happens, it is important to seek help.

Much of this happened to me. As I told you, one of my million-dollar dreams was to play professional baseball. In the fall of 2002 I attended the Division I college that had signed me to play. Fall baseball started immediately, and even though I still had not fully recovered from broken ribs suffered in summer ball, I pushed myself and gave 100% percent and was doing quite well. Then Scout Day was upon us. Being who I am, and having always in the past had to prove my ability, you know that I was going to push myself to be the best I could possibly be in front of all these major league scouts. Even though scouts do not typically attend these games to look at the newcomers, and are most often there to look at the older players that they can actually sign at the end of the year, that didn't matter to me. I wanted to stand out and have them take notice, and unfortunately, they did!

My first at-bat I hit a slow grounder to third base, but I was determined to show off my speed and beat it out. I was always very quick from home to first, but today I was really moving, and I ran like a freight train down to first base. I knew I was about to beat out the play when the first baseman crossed the baseline, and I ran right into him. As I have said previously, I am 5'8" and only 160 pounds. This guy was huge compared to me, and I bounced off of him like a ball bounces off the wall. I hit the ground with a huge crack and lay there looking at my arm and shoulder which was now lying across the front of my body. There was no trainer or medical person in the dugout so I lay on the field for what seemed to be hours in the most excruciating pain I have ever been in. Finally after 20 minutes the coaches wanted to get the game underway and decided to try to move me to the dugout. There, one of the coaches tried to hold my arm in place until the trainer arrived to get me to the hospital.

My dreams were shattered, along with my shoulder, and I was devastated. I experienced great self-pity at my loss. When I began having difficulty with my shoulder not healing properly, I began to blame the college, coaches and trainer for leaving my shoulder out of place for so long, which caused significant irreparable damage. And then, I just plain got angry. I was angry with everyone and everything. What was I to do now? The dream I had been pursuing all my life was gone.

At that time I could have slipped into a great depression. I did a lot of searching and evaluating, and a quote by Tom Smith from the book, *Seabiscuit*, reminded me, *"You don't throw away a whole life just because he's banged up a little."* I knew that this was true; and even though this was a huge setback for me, I also knew that there must be a reason. There must be something else that I was meant to do with my life. Another quote that helped me realize this was something Alexander Graham Bell said, *"When one door closes, another door opens; but we often look so long and so regretfully upon the closed door, that we do not see the ones which open for us."* I made the choice to re-evaluate and take on some new goals. At that point I was determined to find the other open door.

A story that might help illustrate this even better is one I received through an e-mail and later found on the web. I am uncertain of its origin or author, but I believe it's worth repeating.

Shake It Off

One day a farmer's donkey carelessly stumbled into a well. The animal cried piteously for hours as the farmer tried to figure out what to do. Finally he decided the animal was old, and the well needed to be covered up anyway, it just wasn't worth it to retrieve the donkey. He invited all his neighbors to come over and help him. They all grabbed a shovel and began to shovel dirt into the well. At first, the donkey realized what was happening and cried horribly.

Then, to everyone's amazement, he quieted down. A few shovel loads later, the farmer finally looked down the well and was astonished at what he saw. With every shovel of dirt that hit his back, the donkey was doing something amazing. He would shake it off and take a step up. As the farmer's neighbors continued to shovel dirt on top of the animal, he would shake it off and take a step up. Pretty soon, everyone was amazed as the donkey stepped up over the edge of the well and trotted off!

Unknown[5]

As I read this story I could just imagine the donkey wailing with self-pity after falling into the well. As he stood at the bottom of the dark pit he was in, he most likely blamed the farmer for his situation. *If the farmer had taken care of this well I would never have fallen into it. It's all his fault.* When the farmer failed to get him out, I'm sure the donkey was very angry with him, cursing him for his inaction. Soon all was quiet above while the farmer left to enlist the help of his neighbors. As the donkey sat alone in the dark, he began to see his situation for what it really was. With that he became saddened and depressed. Soon dirt began falling into the well onto the donkey, and he realized that he was going to be buried alive. The donkey had two choices. 1) To let his setback consume him and kill him, or 2) to re-evaluate his situation, set a new goal to get out of the well, and take action toward it—action that would change the outcome of his life. He looked for the open door and found it.

Life is going to shovel dirt on you now and then through setbacks, but you cannot allow those setbacks to stop you from pursuing your dreams (even though you may have to change or adjust them). This is when strength of character is developed the most. This is when you will find that you cannot control every factor in life, but you *can* control how you react to it. This is where you will find that there are other ways of achieving your dreams. Or better yet, you will develop more amazing dreams than the ones that you had originally dreamed about. In every difficulty and setback there is great opportunity.

As I said previously there are different ways to react to setbacks. The first is that it may *force you to take a different direction or work harder in order to reach the same goal.*

Michael Jordan had dreams of playing professional basketball but was cut from his high school basketball team! He stated, *"When I got cut from the varsity team as a sophomore in high school, I learned something. I knew I never wanted to feel that bad again. I never wanted to have that taste in my mouth, that hole in my stomach. So I set a goal of becoming a starter on the varsity."* He saw an opportunity in his setback that pushed him to become what many consider the greatest basketball player ever.

In other cases a setback might *force you to make changes to your goal so that it is similar, but not exactly as you had originally planned.*

Oprah Winfrey had dreams of becoming a television news anchorwoman. She worked hard to pursue this goal, and finally got a job. Soon, however, she was let go. She could have continued on the same path and worked harder to achieve this goal, but instead made a few changes to her dreams so that they were similar, but not exactly as she had originally planned. She tweaked her dreams and set her sights on becoming a talk show host. We all know how this story ended. *The Oprah Winfrey Show* is the number one talk show on TV. Her setback led to an even greater opportunity—an opportunity that she probably didn't even originally consider. But because of her setback and appropriate changes to her dreams, she has become one of the most popular women in the world and has changed millions of lives with her positive attitude and inspiration, and she has become a billionaire in the process.

Finally some setbacks *make you completely re-evaluate your goal, and take on new goals.* This, too, can be a wonderful opportunity. Who knew that Frank Sinatra had a hemorrhaged vocal cord and voice problems, so he set his goals on acting? Due to disappointing back-to-back movie flops, Sinatra decided to change his goals and the course of history. Two hundred and forty albums and 2,000 songs later, Frank Sinatra became a singing legend of the twentieth century.

These perceived setbacks all led to greater dreams and greater opportunities. Norman Vincent Peale tells us to, *"Become a possibilitarian. No matter how dark things seem to be or actually are, raise your sights and see possibilities – always see them; for they are always there."* Opportunities and possibilities *are* always there. They are all around us, but many are disguised as setbacks. It is important for you to keep your eyes open, your focus on your goals, and seek that open door or window.

You should also be aware that it is a well-known fact that sometimes the worst thing that happens to you can also become the best thing that happens to you. Someone going through a divorce or losing a job might see that as the worst thing that has happened to them, yet in time, after finding the person of their dreams or a better job, it would appear that it was the best thing that happened to them. The next time something bad happens to you, try to put it in a different perspective and find the positive in it. There is always a positive side to every negative situation, you just have to recognize it. Tell yourself that there is something better for you just around the corner.

Million-Dollar Thoughts

Blinders prevent racehorses from seeing what is all around them, giving them tunnel vision to see only their existing goals. While this may be good in some cases, it doesn't help when it comes to setbacks. Have you experienced a setback that is blinding you to the unlimited possibilities all around you? If so, maybe it is time to re-think your goals and realize that it just might be possible that you haven't dreamed your *greatest* million-dollar dream yet. Take your blinders off and explore this possibility.

Million-Dollar Affirmation

I see numerous opportunities in every difficulty.

Million-Dollar Action

Describe a setback, a negative event or failure that you thought was the worst thing that ever happened to you?

_____

_____

_____

_____

Now find something positive (an opportunity) that came from that event? _____

_____

_____

_____

Chapter 7

Million-Dollar Networking

"The men who have done big things are those who were not afraid to attempt big things, who were not afraid to risk failure in order to gain success."
B.C. Forbes

What exactly is networking? The dictionary defines it as, *"a supportive system of sharing information and services among individuals and groups having a common interest."*[6] In short it is about developing relationships. Networking gives you the opportunity to learn about other people, and puts their knowledge and wisdom at your fingertips from that point on. It's an investment, if nurtured properly, with endless benefits and rewards.

It has been said that there is a chain of no more than six people that links every person on the planet to every other person. This is a profound thought that basically means no person is inaccessible to you. But there is no way to find out if this is actually true until you begin to practice the art of networking. I don't believe in limiting networking to only business, however. I believe networking should be applied to all areas of your life.

Throughout your life you are given an infinite amount of opportunities to network, yet many go unnoticed and not pursued because you might think this concept only applies to work-related efforts. But you will never know if the person standing beside you in a line at the store, on the elevator, or at a sporting event is someone who might present an opportunity that might make a difference in your life unless you open your mouth and speak to him or her.

Life offers a constant exchange of information and knowledge if you only open your eyes to recognize the opportunity. When you do, you will find that wonderful things come from it. Daring to push beyond your comfort zone, and daring to contact people can change your life. This contact doesn't always have to be in person. Using the phone, writing a letter, and using the Internet all work as well.

When I was 14 years old there was a rookie baseball player I was researching. He was in the minor leagues, but I thought he had potential, so I started buying his baseball cards. After attending the one and only game in which I had ever seen him play, I decided to write him a letter of encouragement. Because I didn't have his personal address, I sent the letter to his attention at the baseball club that he was employed by, the Bowie Baysox. Approximately one week later I received a call – a call from him! He was very nice and thanked me for my support and said he hoped my dreams of playing ball would also come true like his were for him. It was an exciting experience for me. Soon after that, the Baltimore Orioles called this player up to the majors!

I also never hesitated writing general managers of professional teams, other professional athletes, or business leaders if I thought I had something to contribute. I never contacted them asking them to do anything. I only contacted them if I thought I could do something for them. Sometimes it was as simple as a thought or idea I had. Granted, some of these people I never heard back from, but others wrote back with encouraging letters, and still others communicated back and forth on several occasions.

What does it hurt to try to reach out to people? But more importantly, what does it hurt if you never try? Without trying you may never get that opportunity to speak to someone, to have someone reply, to learn something new, or even better—a chance to network and build a relationship.

When I was 15 years old I began trading many of my baseball cards on Ebay. At the time, the Banas brothers were two of the most respected sport card dealers, and I decided to contact them. We made a few deals and began communicating. There were very few people on the Internet who knew how old I actually was, but I was up-front with them. I realized this could backfire or could develop into a very good business relationship. Even though they were 12 years my senior, they didn't seem to care about my age, respected my knowledge, and soon were pursuing joint ventures with me. Steve Banas said, *"Kris's age had nothing to do with it. We could tell how enthusiastic he was and we knew he was someone we wanted to network with."*

Over the next five years we did hundreds of deals together. Together these brothers soon built a huge trading card company. Last year I was the biggest distributor of their tennis cards. Not only do we continue to do many joint deals, but we are also friends and act as business sounding boards for each other. When I have ideas, I bounce them off of them. When they have ideas, they do the same with me. We are able to go back and forth until an idea is perfected, utilizing our combined knowledge, expertise and experience. This has been an invaluable relationship built by a simple networking opportunity.

Networking is actually fun because you never know where one conversation, letter, or contact will lead. I have met some of the most interesting people due to chance meetings, or by stretching a bit and going to places that others my age don't typically go.

As an example I decided to stretch a bit and extend my sport card business worldwide, which led to my meeting and working with people in Japan, France, Germany, Australia and other distant countries. I have learned so much from these contacts. Also, since my injury and refocusing of my goals I have begun attending business meetings that are typically only for established businessmen. Yes I'm the only person under the age of 25, 30 or even 35, but I don't care. I learn from the monthly meetings by listening to the incredible business speakers who come to the meetings. This has given me the opportunity to meet and have lunch with some sport powerhouses like Pat Williams, Senior Vice President of the Orlando Magic *(who was also kind enough to write the foreword to this book when I asked him)*, former baseball greats like Sudden Sam McDowell and Wade Boggs, and former New England Patriot, Keith Lee, to name a few. I have made a few very good contacts that genuinely seem to be interested in my growth and progress; and I have had the opportunity to improve my networking and communication skills for the future.

Dale Carnegie, founder of Dale Carnegie Training, has helped people improve their communication and leadership skills for over 90 years. In Carnegie's book, *How To Win Friends and Influence People,* he discusses a study conducted that showed that 85% of a person's career success depended on his or her ability to relate and interact with other people: network. Some other interesting statistics showed that 70% of all jobs are found through networking, and on the average, you'll make 15 to 25 face-to-face contacts per day. Non-direct contact, such as Internet connections, could be in the thousands. Again, our ability to network with new people is there for the taking.

You might be reading this and be thinking to yourself, *"What if I'm not as outgoing as you are? It might be easy for you, but not for me."* Whether you want to believe it or not, I'm actually a really shy individual. I have quite a bit of self-confidence in networking when it comes to the Internet or writing, but face to face is more difficult for me. Knowing this, however, makes me work at it harder. I have to challenge myself to get out of my comfort zone to make new face-to-face contacts. It's not always easy, but I keep in mind that good networkers are not born, they are made. It takes effort, and it takes action on my part. It doesn't come easy, but it is worth it. That's why I continue to do it.

Think about some of the most successful business people that you know, the most successful athletes, and the most successful actors. What do they all have in common? They all promote themselves through networking. If they didn't, they wouldn't accomplish all that they want to accomplish. Basically if someone painted a beautiful picture, but didn't network and tell others about it, they would never sell it. An actor would never be known as a great actor without auditioning and showing others what he or she can do. The same goes for athletes or businesspeople. How successful would a salesman be if he didn't interact with people who might buy from him?

Let's begin with the basics of networking in order to get you started on a path of unlimited contacts and opportunities.

1) Choose good networking opportunities. There are numerous business or school clubs and events to make good contacts. Look for events that specifically target those people that you would most like to network with. Also try and find events that are set up to allow effective networking time. Then simply attend and look for people who are by themselves or look like they are looking for someone to speak with, too. You will find that a lot of people find this type of function uncomfortable and will be thankful to have someone to talk to.

2) Be prepared to network at unexpected times. Like I said before, networking isn't always a scheduled item on your calendar. Opportunities to network take place everywhere and at very unexpected times. Don't be a bystander in your life. Be aware of your surroundings at all times, and you will notice how many people cross your path and give you the opportunity to connect. Smiling at people you meet is always a good start. The second act might be to say hello. The third would be to comment on your surroundings or the reason that you are both in the same place at the same time. See if that starts a conversation. If nothing else comes of the conversation, at least you were nice to one person you met during the day.

3) Be prepared to reach out to the perceived unreachable. There are many successful people in this world that you may be intimidated by for one reason or another. You may think these people are unapproachable due to their status or success. As examples, how many people might write to Donald Trump, Malcolm Forbes or Michael Jordan? Maybe a small percentage might take the chance to network with someone like this, but by doing so you have nothing to lose and everything to gain. Don't limit who you are willing to network with by letting your preconceived notions tell you that they are unapproachable and would not want to network with you.

4) Be a good listener. Once you actually start getting out there and networking with other people you will find that people LOVE to talk about themselves. But keep in mind, we were given two ears and one mouth for a reason – so that we can listen twice as much as we speak. Effective networkers have mastered the art of listening by asking good questions and then listening to the answers. By doing this you will hear what people need, and then you will be able to help them more effectively.

5) Give before receiving. You should approach every networking opportunity with the attitude of, *what can I do for you—not what can you do for me.* When you place the needs of others before your needs, you will find that you are rewarded. It also gives you the benefit of helping someone else, which is one of the main reasons we are here—to help others.

6) Be Honest. Sincerity can be spotted a mile away, as can insincerity. The moment you meet someone they begin to form an opinion of you. They decide whether or not you are the type of person they would like to continue to build a relationship with. Your reputation, and reputation for honesty, is of utmost importance.

7) Follow up. To complete the networking process, you must always follow up with the individual you have spoken with. Continual follow-up is necessary in order to start building trust and a relationship. It takes time, energy, and patience to see the long-term effects and benefits; however, all of this will ultimately be worth it to further your goals and success.

8) Build a Networking Dream Team. Develop relationships with key advisors who can help you personally and who can also introduce you to others. It pays to have good legal and tax specialists and other consultants on your team. Also remember to deal with specialists. Don't hire a real estate attorney to put together a contract to play baseball. Find a good firm with a number of experts and become known to them.

People with million-dollar dreams cannot typically achieve them alone. It will almost always take networking to build a dream team: a group of people all committed to seeing you succeed in the pursuit of your dreams. Effective networking will help to create such a team, and will also give you the opportunity to be on other people's dream teams to help them.

Million-Dollar Thoughts

When was the last time you met someone new? When was the last time you attended a function that you don't normally attend? If you want to achieve your million-dollar dreams, you realize that you cannot stay hidden among your current friends and family. You realize you must expand the network of people you know and interact with. What has held you back from doing this in the past? To face a fear is often to defeat that fear. Visualize meeting and striking up conversations with person after person. Then when the opportunity arises, you will be well prepared to open your mouth and begin speaking.

Million-Dollar Affirmation

I seek out opportunities to network in
all areas of my life.

Million-Dollar Action

In the next week list five places that you will go. (ie: work, a little league game, a school event, the grocery store etc.)

_____

_____

_____

_____

_____

Make it a point to speak to one person that you normally do not speak to at each place.

Chapter 8

Million-Dollar Risk Taking

"Change and growth take place when a person has risked himself and dares to become involved with experimenting with his own life."
Herbert A. Otto

One of my favorite quotes is written on a baseball picture that is framed and hangs above my desk, *"You can't steal second base and keep your foot on first."* (Frederick B. Wilcox)

Rickey Henderson, nicknamed *Man of Steal*, holds the most records for steals in baseball, along with a single-season base stealing record of 130 set in 1982. In 1991 he broke Lou Brock's all-time record of 938 steals, and through 2003 had 1,406 stolen bases. Without risking the possibility of being thrown out, this would never have happened.

Babe Ruth is probably one of the best-known baseball players due to his home run hitting ability. He hit 714 home runs in his career, but struck out 1,330 times. Was he known as the strikeout king? No, the *Sultan of Swat* was known for his home runs. Ruth didn't let the fear of striking out get in the way of his goals, but it took risk. Every time he was up at bat, he risked striking out. But the way Ruth looked at it was, *"Every strike brings me closer to the next home run."* Hank Aaron, who topped Ruth's record by hitting 755 home runs, felt the same way. *"My motto was always to keep swinging,"* said Aaron.

These baseball greats, and others like them, were willing to step up to the plate and take the risks necessary to succeed. For many people, that risk is just too great. They would rather stay in their comfort zone and give up any potential reward rather than strike out at what they are doing. They are so afraid of losing that they never win. Successful people with million-dollar dreams all share one common trait—they are willing to step up to the plate, swing for the fences, steal the base, and take the risk necessary for success.

If you are honest with yourself, you may find that you are pretty comfortable in the comfort zone you have created for yourself. It is a safe and non-threatening place to be. But staying there trades the challenge of reaching your million-dollar dreams for mediocrity. Once you are willing to settle for mediocrity in one area of your life, you are prone to settle in other significant ways. Even though the comfort zone is a seductive place to stay, the inability to step out will forever hinder your ability to become all that you are meant to be. You've heard the old saying, *"nothing ventured, nothing gained."* When you don't venture out and risk achieving your million-dollar dreams, you have already failed. Because when you fail to try, you fail – period!

This stepping out of your comfort zone, however, is simply growth. Picture a child learning to walk. Step after step he falls down. He gets up, tries again, and falls down again. If he decided to stay in his comfort zone, he would decide to crawl around forever and forget his dream of walking. A baby, however, doesn't fear growth and continues to pursue his dream. After numerous *failures*, he finally succeeds and reaches his goal and walks across the floor. George Shinn, owner of the Charlotte Hornets NBA basketball team, stated, *"Growth means change, and change involves risk, stepping from the known to the unknown."*

Growth can be scary because there is often great fear associated with it. Without fear there would only be optimism, hope, encouragement and pursuit of dreams. With it there is procrastination, pessimism, destitution and the paralysis of dreams. Look what the terrorist acts of September 11, 2001, did to the people of the United States. It paralyzed them with fear—fear of traveling, fear of more attacks, fear of pursuing their dreams. People's lives froze. They struggled to *get back to business* as the President of the country insisted. They were glued to their TV in antici-pation of the next attack. Many confessed they could not seem to go forward with their lives. It was as if this fear had sapped all of their energy from their bodies. This fear far exceeded most people's comfort zone, but many people feel these same responses from the fear of rejection, humiliation, and failure.

It is obvious that fear is incredibly powerful, but the key to overcoming it is to respond to it effectively. Reclaiming your life from fear means breaking the habits that feed the problem. You must make this a realistic choice. You don't have to let fear prevent you from achieving your million-dollar dreams. You can triumph over it once you face it squarely in the eyes, because a fear faced is a defeated one.

An old saying goes, *"Boats are safe anchored in the harbor, but that's not what boats are made for."* You were not made for living your life safely, but living fearlessly does not happen all at once. Change takes place inch by inch, and when you focus on inches (small changes), you will start to move forward. This positive action begins to move you from where you are, to where you want to be— achieving your million-dollar dreams.

Recognizing that much of your comfort zone is created by groundless fears, you can begin to start taking small risks. Think back to your first date. How long did it take you to get up the courage to ask the person out? When you start to analyze the situation for what it is, you find the following: 1) If you don't ask, you'll never go out on a date. 2) If you do ask, the worst thing that can happen is that he or she says no, and you are no worse off than when you started, but 3) if you do ask, he or she might say yes! Once you realize the downside and the potential, the choice should be pretty clear. Keep in mind that where there is risk, there is also reward.

I had to go through this same process when, in order to pursue my dreams, I was debating whether or not I wanted to leave a town where I grew up, knew everyone, and was comfortable. I had to decide if I was willing to leave all my friends and not enjoy senior year with them. I had to decide if I was willing to step into a new school four times bigger than my old school without knowing anyone. And I also had to decide if I was willing to go from being one of the best baseball players in Maine to being an unknown in Florida. I weighed the risks and rewards and asked my parents to consider the move. After a lot of deliberation, my family made the move from Maine to Florida.

For every risk there is a reward, but you will never know what that reward is unless you take the risk. Granted not all risks are worth it, but if they relate to your million-dollar dreams, they just might be. But be practical and smart about your risk-taking. Would skydiving without a parachute be a good risk? Probably not, but would taking a loan from the bank to begin your dream business be a good risk? It just might be. Successful risk-takers take calculated risks, not crazy ones! When calculating your risk, you must know the chances of success, the potential rewards, and, of course, the consequences of failure. But taking risks is an opportunity to stretch and venture into new areas. It means you are allowing yourself an opportunity to achieve something greater than you have before. T.S. Eliot said, *"Only those who will risk going too far can possibly find out how far one can go."* You will never know what greatness you are destined for without taking some risk to find out.

Sometimes, however, you will take risks that end up not working to your advantage, or do not accomplish what you had hoped they would. Remember Babe Ruth? He tried to hit over 2,000 home runs and struck out 1,330 of those times trying! But people don't remember those 1,330 times. They remember the 714 times he actually did achieve his goals. Whenever you seek to accomplish million-dollar dreams, which may or may not include fame, fortune or excellence, you place yourself at risk. B.C. Forbes clearly states, *"The men who have done big things are those who were not afraid to attempt big things, who were not afraid to risk failure in order to gain success."* He was clearly one of these men who risked failure to attempt big things. When you do this, however, you *will* fail more, but you have to learn from those failures and look at them as stepping-stones to your success.

Have I ever taken a risk that didn't prove successful? Anyone with million-dollar financial goals like I have knows the importance of investing his or her money. Placing money under a mattress or in a non-interest-bearing checking account will obviously not help to accomplish financial goals. It is important to invest your money, and there are numerous ways to do this. I chose to invest in my business, in the stock market, and in a few private deals. Some of these avenues of investment have been very profitable, while others have not. There have been times when I made nice profits on stocks, and other times when I lost my shirt on them. But when you weigh all the risks and all the losses versus the ultimate rewards and gains, I definitely came out a lot better than if I had never invested at all. Yes I've definitely taken risks that didn't prove successful. But I didn't give up and crawl back to my comfort zone of my first savings account and stop investing. I know that I have to continue to invest and continue to learn in order to move toward my goals.

The most successful people in this world are persistent risk-takers. You must learn to become one as well. Risk-taking is the key element that allows you to live life to its fullest and achieve all that you are meant to achieve. Then, and only then, will you achieve your million-dollar dreams. Helen Keller said it best, *"Life is either a daring adventure or nothing at all"*.

Million-Dollar Thoughts

Recall a time when you stepped out of your comfort zone to pursue something of importance to you. Maybe it was the day you asked your girl to marry you, or maybe it was the day you quit a dead-end job to pursue a better one. Whatever it was, how did it make you feel when your risk paid off? Hold on to this successful feeling, and use it each time you begin to think about taking a new risk that moves you toward your million-dollar dreams.

Million-Dollar Affirmation

I step out of my comfort zone in order to pursue the risks necessary to achieve my million-dollar dreams.

Million-Dollar Action

Describe a risk that you need to take in order to achieve your million-dollar dreams.

_____

_____

_____

What is the worst thing that can happen if you do this?

_____

_____

What is the best thing that can happen if you do this?

_____

_____

Chapter 9

Million-Dollar
Responsibilities

"In helping others, we shall help ourselves,
for whatever good we give out completes the circle
and comes back to us."
Flora Edwards

Million-dollar dreams are not achieved alone. I'm certain that all successful people will tell you that there were numerous others who helped them to achieve their dreams. The help may have come from a businessperson sharing his or her expertise, or the teacher sharing his or her knowledge. It may have been a banker, or friend's financial commitment or loan. Or it could have been something as simple as encouragement from his or her parents, or a spouse who believed in their dreams. Whatever it was you must recognize that all these people played an important role in their success. It never was a one-man (or woman) effort.

Many people helped me, and continue to help me along the way to reaching my million-dollar dreams. First and foremost, there is my mother, my father and my sister Kaily. Without their endless support and belief in me, I wouldn't be the person I am today. I was also lucky enough to have the support of all four of my grandparents. They cheered me on both on, and off the field. The list of people who have supported me, believed in me, and helped me in one way or another is endless, as I'm sure it is for you. Wilma Rudolph recognized that this is always the case when she said, *"No matter what great things you accomplish, somebody helps you."* No one succeeds and reaches his or her goals alone. There are always people helping you along the way.

I also believe God plays an important role in helping you to achieve your dreams. When things all come together like clock-work, or when that big break happens at the right time, some might think they are coincidences, but I believe that there is a greater power working behind the scenes to help you on your way. I have experienced this personally in my life and have found that many other successful people have as well. When I first created and went live with my website, *www.athletesuccess.com*, I invited people to share their stories of setbacks and successes. Numerous stories came in, each sharing their innermost thoughts, but the similar theme in all of them was that in order to find true success, not simply material success, they had to get their priorities straight. They all found a need to put God first; and once they did, then they experienced the success and happiness they were seeking. You obviously need to practice your own faith and beliefs, but mine is that all things are possible *with* God—not without.

Just like other people help you to reach your goals and dreams, you should also help others reach theirs. You don't have to wait until you achieve your dreams in order to help people though. If you do that, you might miss numerous opportunities to help when your help is most needed. When an opportunity arises, help as you can. When you achieve your million-dollar dreams, keep in mind the following Bible quote from Luke 12:48, *"To whom much is given, much is expected."* But what does it mean? I think others have answered that question much better than I ever could.

"A life isn't significant except for its impact
on other lives."
Jackie Robinson

"Success has nothing to do with what you gain
in life or accomplish for yourself.
It's what you do for others."
Danny Thomas

"Successful people are always looking for
opportunities to help others."
Brian Tracy

*"What we have done for ourselves alone dies with us;
what we have done for others and the
world remains and is immortal."*
Albert Pike

*"We make a living by what we get.
We make a life by what we give."*
Winston Churchill

*"The wise person understands that his own happiness
must include the happiness of others."*
Dennis Weaver

*"Never underestimate what a simple gesture can do. It is
the little things that you do that make a big
difference in other people's lives."*
Catherine Pulsifer

*"We are not put on this earth for ourselves,
but are placed here for each other. If you are there always
for others, then in time of need,
someone will be there for you."*
Jeff Warner

The main point is that whatever you do in life should help others and affect them in a positive manner. When you are fortunate enough to experience success, it is your responsibility to share it. You can do this by sharing your knowledge, your wisdom, and your experience with others. You can share your special talents and abilities with those who are in need. You can share your financial resources. But most of all, you can share yourself as only you can uniquely do. You can share your praise, your encouragement, and your love.

An example of someone who did this was Princess Diana. Even though her life was far from perfect, she lived a life that offered her privileges that few people shared. She decided to use these privileges to help others less fortunate than she was. She used her media popularity to bring attention to several charitable causes, including AIDS. By showing love and compassion through acts as simple as a smile, a word of encouragement, or a hug, it greatly affected the lives of those she touched. Through her example, others followed. Today her work continues to motivate others to follow in her footsteps and donate their time to helping others.

Every day we hear about celebrities, such as actors or athletes, who are donating their time and money to various causes. Because of their ability to attract media coverage their efforts reap big results for those they are helping. Behind the scenes successful businesspeople, teachers and professors are training and mentoring young entrepreneurs and helping them up the ladder of success. But even more quietly is the day to day interaction that each and every one of us is having with every person we come in contact with. We all have the ability to help others and share ourselves. It might be as simple as giving a waitress a bigger tip, encouraging a friend's dreams, babysitting while a neighbor pursues her education, or helping an elderly person write a letter to his or her friends or children. There will be many opportunities to share with others. You simply have to keep your eyes open in order to recognize all the opportunities that you are presented with. The part that your eyes will not see, however, is the ripple effect of your actions. Every time you give of yourself, you set an example for others to do the same.

There is another area of responsibility that is critical to your continued success. When you achieve your dreams, you should, as Brian Tracy stated, *"Develop an attitude of gratitude, and give thanks for everything that happens to you, knowing that every step forward is a step toward achieving something bigger and better than your current situation."* There is one human trait that scientists, philosophers and all the world's major religions agree upon, and that is gratitude. They believe it to be a morally beneficial emotional state. According to scientific research gratitude makes you healthier, more alert, enthusiastic, determined, more attentive and energetic. So what do you think these traits will do for you? Of course they will help you to continue pursuing your dreams.

As a society we have become distracted and unmoved by the everyday wonders around us. Robert Louis Stevenson once noted that the person who *"has forgotten to be thankful has fallen asleep in the midst of life."* We have become an apathetic society that fails to notice all of the miracles taking place around us. We may watch the change of seasons or the sun rise and set, yet we appear to be unmoved. We may take for granted the referral we get from a friend that moves us closer to our goal, or we may take for granted the hard work of our spouse, partner or employee who are all behind the scenes helping us to reach our goals. Expressing gratitude is the antidote to this complacency. Once you take your blinders off you begin to recognize all of the people and all of the events for which you actually can be grateful.

The practice of gratitude is a state of mind and a state of awareness. You need to open your eyes and be thankful for everything in your life. Gratitude is something that you cannot give to excess. It helps you grow as a person and reminds you to take nothing in your life for granted. It is a true trait of a successful person who is pursuing his or her million-dollar dreams.

Million-Dollar Thoughts

Before going to sleep tonight practice the art of gratefulness. Be sincerely thankful for everything in your life—present and past.

Million-Dollar Affirmation

I am grateful for those in my life and recognize their importance. I also recognize my importance in other's lives and seek opportunities to enrich their lives further.

Million-Dollar Action

List three of the most influential and helpful people in your life for whom you are most grateful.

_____

_____

_____

List three instances you have had a positive impact on the lives of others.

_____

_____

_____

How can you create opportunities to do this more frequently?

_____

_____

Chapter 10

Million-Dollar Lifestyle

"Try not to become a man of success but rather to become a man of value."
Albert Einstein

No matter what your million-dollar dreams are, or how different yours may be from mine, we still all tend to strive for a million-dollar life. In the end, you have to decide what this means to you because it means different things to different people. There are, however, some common denominators that most people are inclined to share. Most expect to have happiness, health, financial freedom, good personal relationships and a sense of fulfillment and peace of mind.

Happiness. Fortunately happiness comes from within. There is no external source that can make you happy. You do that yourself by choosing happiness on a day-to-day and hour-to-hour basis. Burton Hills stated, *"Happiness is not a destination. It is a method of life."* Therefore, if this is the case, it should be a given that you already have happiness in your life because it's what you are choosing, or at least it should be.

While I'm far from perfect in this area, it is something I try to remember each morning when I wake up. When I look in the mirror in the morning, I try to remember to choose happiness for the day.

Health. When God was asked in the famous poem, *An Interview With God, "What surprises you most about humankind?"* God's answer was, *"That they lose their health to make money...and then lose their money to restore their health."* This is sad, but true. Often people are so obsessed with making money or achieving their dreams that they forget that taking care of their health needs to be a vital part of this process. Maintaining a high level of physical and mental health needs be one of your top priorities if you are to experience a million-dollar life. Unfortunately, this isn't the statistical case as reported by the Department of Health and Human Services and the National Center for Health Statistics.

- ◆ 66.6% of the U.S. population is overweight.
- ◆ 30.5% are obese.
- ◆ 58% of Americans do not engage in any physical activity.
- ◆ 25% are completely sedentary.
- ◆ Less than 31.8% of U.S. adults get regular leisure time.

- ◆ 25.2 million men and 21.2 million women are smokers.
- ◆ About 62.5% of Americans are drinkers, and 32.4% say they drink more than they should.
- ◆ Alcohol consumption and abuse cost our society $86 billion each year.
- ◆ Sleep experts recommend 8 hours of sleep per night, yet the average adult gets under 7 hours and 33% get only 6 hours or less.
- ◆ Cardiovascular disease is the single leading cause of death in America today.
- ◆ Americans spend 1.4 trillion dollars on health expenditures each year

It is obvious with statistics such as these that we, as a society, are not making our health a priority. It makes no sense to put the effort into achieving your dreams if you are to lose your health in the process; therefore, keeping your health has to be part of your million-dollar dream. Obviously there are simple practices that can help you to do this such as not smoking, not drinking in excess, and not taking drugs. But you also need to focus on your eating and exercise habits, and your sleeping and relaxation patterns.

Take the time to analyze your diet and consume foods that benefit your body such as whole grains, fruits and vegetables, and chicken and fish. Try to stay away from overly processed foods, man-made foods, sugar and white flour products. If you are uncertain as to where to begin in this area, I would recommend your reading, *The Body By God*, by Dr. Ben Lerner. Also, keep your body hydrated by drinking plenty of water.

Exercise is also critical to your health. It has been proven that it has numerous advantages such as it can lower blood pressure and cholesterol, reduce stress, keep you at a good weight, and add years to your life. Do at least 30-45 minutes of active exercise 3-4 times a week. You can do this in any form such as walking, swimming, playing sports or going to the gym. Do whatever you enjoy the best.

Besides exercising, make sure you get your eight hours of sleep. Sleeping is when the body rejuvenates itself. Don't cut yourself short in this area. And finally, as important as sleep is to your body, relaxation is to your mind. Take the time each day to relax—even if it is only for a ½ hour per day. Find some alone time and rest your mind. I also believe that it is important to take time away from work and your daily routines in the form of vacations whenever you can. This doesn't have to be in the form of elaborate, expensive trips. It can be as simple as taking a couple days off and taking day trips, going for walks, or relaxing on the beach. When John F. Kennedy's father was asked how he started to become successful, he replied, *"When I stopped pushing for it, and went up and sat on the Cape and gave myself time to think."*

Time to clear your head from the hustle and bustle of the day will not put you behind as you might think, but instead help you to move forward more efficiently.

My health has always been important me as I am sure it is to any athlete. Keeping my body healthy with exercise, good food, rest and relaxation has always been a priority for me. Even though there are times when you don't have control over what happens to your body (such as a car accident or being exposed to a contagious disease), if your body is initially pretty healthy, it will be easier for you to overcome these outside factors that may affect you.

Financial Freedom. Everyone desires financial freedom, and most think the only way to obtain it is by winning the lottery or getting a huge inheritance. But financial freedom is not just having a big lump sum of money. It is living within your means and not beyond them. For some, financial freedom might come at $30,000 a year, whereas for others it might be $150,000 a year. Everyone's financial freedom comes at a different price. I've already discussed a lot about finances and spending previously, so all I will add to it is that money doesn't buy happiness, and spending beyond your means *definitely* will not cause happiness. Managing your funds realistically and appropriately is the best way to achieve financial freedom.

Personal Relationships. People need good personal relationships in order to have a well-balanced, healthy personality.

◆ The primary relationships that most people have are with their families. These relationships should be of utmost importance, positive and cultivated to make them even better.

♦ Second to family are friendships. Unlike family, you get to choose your friends. Choose people who are supportive and enhance your life.

♦ Then there are your business relationships that are very powerful and can render negative or positive experiences for you. Seek an environment of business relationships that work together and encourage growth and success rather than competition and repression.

♦ Finally there is your relationship with your community, which includes your neighborhood, the people in your town, the clubs you belong to and everyone else that you meet along the way. Leave a lasting impression on all of these people that you are someone who cares.

Nothing can bring more happiness to your life than good relationships. Cheryl Richardson, author of *Take Time For Your Life*, states, *"The depth of meaning, understanding and appreciation that these kinds of relationships bring is almost unfathomable."* Start building good relationships today.

Peace of Mind. Most people believe that external conditions can bring about happiness and peace of mind, but peace of mind only comes from within. It begins with a sense of contentment, and shows up by being happy with who you are and what you represent. It is a sense of fulfillment, comfort, and belief that your life is on the right track.

But believing in, and placing your trust in something greater and more powerful than you is also essential to having peace of mind. Faith is powerful. When you realize that you were created for a reason, and have all the tools and resources necessary to become the person to fulfill that purpose, there is no need for worry or concern, and then you can experience an even greater sense of peace.

Peace of mind begins when you stop worrying about the future and stop regretting the past. It is the reward you receive when you start living in the present. When you think about it, you cannot change the past, so why dwell there. You also cannot live in the future because it simply becomes the present when it arrives. Babatunde Olatunji stated, "*Yesterday is history. Tomorrow is a mystery. And today? Today is a gift. That's why we call it the present.*" When we accept today as a gift and live in the present and realize that our life is on track, that is when and where we will find peace of mind.

I actually struggled with this for quite awhile. After my baseball accident I continually kept looking back at the past questioning *why*. I would replay the day I dislocated my shoulder over and over in my head and say *what if*. I wanted to change what had happened to me so much that I couldn't live in the present because I was consumed with the events of that one day, one hour, one minute of my life. When I wasn't thinking about the past, I would look to the future and say, *now what?* This wasn't a very peaceful time for me. Peace of mind didn't begin for me until I began to re-evaluate my life, set new goals and begin to live in the present. When I started focusing on one day at a time, and living that day to my full potential doing things that brought me closer to my new goals, it felt like I was renewed and healed somehow. It was at that time that I began to feel happy again and at peace with my life.

While you might not feel that this is an important aspect to your life, I think it is one of the most important. You have to like yourself and what you are doing on a day-to-day basis and feel good about it all. And when you do, you'll find that this feeling alone can do wonders to help you achieve your dreams. Because you will be living each day in the present, maximizing that day, not wasting it on the past or future, you will find that you are more productive, more positive, and are moving more quickly toward the achievement of your dreams.

Take the time to seriously evaluate whether or not you are living the million-dollar life, and take the steps necessary to make sure you do.

Million-Dollar Thoughts

If you were living a million-dollar life, what would it look like? What would you be doing to maintain a great level of health and happiness? What would your eating and exercise habits be like? What would your personal relationships be like? How does this image differ from your current reality?

Million-Dollar Affirmation

I am happy and have peace of mind because I know I am doing what is necessary to live a million-dollar life.

Million-Dollar Action

List as many new exercise, eating and health habits that are necessary to achieve your million-dollar life.

_____

_____

_____

_____

_____

List ways in which you can improve your relationships with your family, spouse and friends that will bring you more happiness.

_____

_____

_____

Chapter 11

Million-Dollar Exchange

"Many hands, hearts, and minds generally contribute to anyone's notable achievements."
Walt Disney

Everyone has heard of the New York Stock Exchange. In simplistic terms, it's a place where you can buy or sell (give or get) something of value. The largest and most valuable exchange in the world, however, is the exchange of information. If you want to achieve your million-dollar dreams, you have to become part of this priceless exchange. You will also need to be on both the receiving end as well as the giving end of this transference of knowledge, resources and information.

1) *Exchange of Knowledge*

The word communication comes from the Latin word *communico,* which means to share. There is an abundance of knowledge and experience in the world that others are willing to share with you. It is available to help you succeed in reaching your million-dollar dreams. Many people forget, or don't realize that this wealth of knowledge is available to them, and as a result, try to re-invent the wheel over and over. Instead, learn from others. Make knowledge, professional development and personal growth a priority in your life. Brian Tracy states, *"No one lives long enough to learn everything they need to learn starting from scratch. To be successful, we absolutely, positively have to find people who have already paid the price to learn the things that we need to learn to achieve our goals."*

Thomas Edison also gave us some great advice on this. He said, *"The first thing is to find out everything everybody else knows, and then begin where they left off."* The easiest way to do this is to watch what others are doing, read what others have written, and hear what others have said. Robert E. Lee remarked, *"The education of man is never completed until he dies."* Learning is obviously a lifelong process.

There are literally millions of great books on the shelves of bookstores and libraries that could help you to achieve your dreams. For a few dollars and a few hours, you can learn what it took others years and lifetimes to learn. Statistics show, however, that the average American reads less than one book per year, and 58% of high school graduates never read another book in their lifetimes. It is estimated that 20% of the population reads 80% of the books sold in bookstores. You might be thinking to yourself, *what bookworms or geeks they must be,* but the truth of the matter is that some of the most successful people in America correlate their success to the amount they read. That's probably why self-help and management books are among the best sellers today. Those wanting true success are devouring this information and learning from the masters, which is ultimately helping them to reach their own goals and dreams.

Mark Twain once made the comment, *"The man who does not read good books has no advantage over the man who cannot read them."* Take advantage of this gift you have. Read at least one hour a day. By doing this you will read approximately 50 books a year, which will definitely set you apart from 80% of the population. And with the additional knowledge you obtain from reading, you will be one step closer to accomplishing your dreams.

I personally never had that love of reading. However, when you want to be the best at something and really love whatever it is, you can't feed your brain enough of it. When it came to baseball, that's how I was. I read baseball magazines, books on hitting, throwing, and all aspects of the game. I read books on other players and how they succeeded, the sports pages of the newspapers, and of course, researched baseball information and players nonstop on the Internet. I fed my brain this information daily, and it made a difference—not only in my playing, but my understanding of the game. When you have a million-dollar dream that excites you, you will find that you crave all the information you can get about it. When this is the case, reading is not a chore, but a pleasure.

To help you begin, I'm listing just a few of my favorite non-baseball books that I believe will help propel you more quickly to your dreams.

Hill, Napoleon. Think & Grow Rich. New York: Ballantine, 1987.

Staples, Dr. Walter Doyle. Think Like A Winner! California: Wilshire, 1991.

Mandino, Og. The Greatest Salesman In the World. New York: Bantom, 1968.

Robbins, Anthony. Awaken The Giant Within. New York: Fireside, 1991.

Peale, Norman Vincent. The Power Of Positive Thinking. New Jersey: Prentice-Hall, 1978, 1952.

Canfield, Jack and Mark Victor Hanson. The Aladdin Factor. New York: Berkley, 1995.

Hanson, Mark Victor and Robert G. Allen. One Minute Millionaire. New York: Harmony, 2002.

Trump, Donald J. Trump – How to Get Rich. New York: Random House, 2004.

Tracy, Brian. Maximum Achievement. New York: Fireside, 1995.

McKay, Harvey. <u>Dig Your Well Before You're Thirsty – The Only Networking Book You'll Ever Need</u>. New York: Currency, 1997.

Stoltz, Paul G. Ph.D. <u>Adversity Quotient – Turning Obstacles Into Opportunities</u>. New York: John Wiley, 1997.

2) Exchange of Resources

Reading isn't the only means of exchange. There are other resources such as tapes and CDs. For those of you in the car for hours at a time, listening to a motivation book on self-improvement instead of music can be invaluable. There are also inspirational posters to hang on your wall, and courses on financial planning. All of the following companies offer products designed to inspire you, motivate you, educate you and help you to reach your dreams. Again, these are some of my favorites.

<u>Nightingale Conant</u> – *www.nightingale.com* - The number one resource in the world for motivational and self-improvement audio products.

<u>Dale Carnegie Training</u> – *www.dalecarnegie.com* – Courses and training in creating world-class relationship and speaking skills.

<u>Science For Success</u> - *www.scienceforsuccess.com* – The most up-to-date brain research and how it can help you to succeed.

<u>Successories</u> – *www.successories.com* – Motivational products (such as pictures, posters, mugs) that reinforce your goals.

My parents were always buying me something from Successories and have a full library of tapes from Nightingale Conant. They have proven to be great motivational resources. All of the above are wonderful tools, but don't forget one of my favorite resources – the Internet. The Internet puts an infinite amount of knowledge at your fingertips in seconds and provides an unlimited amount of exchanges between individuals through e-mail, instant-messaging and web-sites. The Internet-Highway is considered the place to go for the greatest exchange of information in the world.

3) Exchange of <u>Your</u> Information

As important as it is to obtain knowledge and information from other people and other resources, it is just as important for you to share what you do and what you know with others. This is where the other side of the exchange takes place. You need to communicate what you do, what you know, and what you need in order to accomplish your million-dollar dreams.

You can do this in many ways. You could write a book like the one I have just written. Through it I'm hoping to accomplish two things: 1) I'm hoping to help others achieve their dreams--especially teens and young-adults. I feel they might be able to relate to me better than to a 50-

year old telling them the same thing, and 2) I'm hoping to set myself apart from the crowd. In less than two years I will graduate with a B.A. in finance, but so will thousands of other people. What will differentiate me from everyone else? Maybe our grades will to a degree, but again, I'm sure there will be thousands with good grades. There has to be something different, something that sets me apart from the crowd, so I'm going out on a limb to try to do that.

I discussed using the Internet. I personally think Ebay is the best tool for exchange in the world. It is literally one of the greatest sources available to let millions know what you have to offer. I started buying and selling collectible cards on Ebay in 1998. By the end of that year, Ebay had their first million members. Today they have over 100 million members. Therefore, whenever I offer a product on Ebay, I have the potential of reaching 100 million people. I'm sure not everyone wants to look at what I have to sell, but many do. Ebay is one of the reasons my collectible business has done so well. It has given me the tool to reach and exchange with more people than I could by using any other method.

Another aspect of Ebay that I particularly like is their customer feedback system. This allows you to view the reputation of those you are doing business with. My reputation is extremely important to me, and I want satisfied customers, because a satisfied customer is a repeat customer. In the thousands of transactions I have conducted over the years I have a 100% customer satisfaction rating. If you are going to build good business relationships, you have to conduct your business at the highest standards you can. Honesty and integrity in all your dealings has to be of utmost importance to you because people will exchange this type of information, especially if it's bad. If you don't care about your customers, trust me, the word will get around.

Along with using someone else's Internet site such as Ebay to exchange information, you also have the ability to have your own website. In 2004 I put up my first website, *www.athletesuccess.com.* In today's world, you really need a web presence. Often the first thing a new acquaintance will ask you is, *"Do you have a website?"* Now I do; and probably so should you. There are so many resources to help you to build a website that there is no longer an excuse not to have one. It used to be that the cost was often prohibitive, and while you can still spend thousands to have a site built for you, you can also get one for virtually the cost of a monthly hosting fee (which I've seen start as low as $3.95 per month).

An effective resource I've found associated with websites is affiliate programs. This exchange of information lets you offer other people's products and services on your site. As an example, on my website I list a few people that I know and trust and describe their services. By clicking on their photo or link, it will take you to their website. This helps them by exposing them to people that go to my site and maybe wouldn't go to theirs. On the other side of this exchange, many people make reference to my site on their website. This is a nice way of people helping people reach more people.

When my dreams of playing professional baseball were shattered, I decided to research all aspects of becoming an athlete agent. I took courses and read as much as I could on the subject, and in 2004 became a licensed athlete agent. I then became affiliated with a company my parents had started, Peak Power Marketing and Management, Inc. (www.peakpowermarketing.com). Being part of this company has taught me the importance of teamwork. I've learned that when everyone works for the common-good of a team, the results and rewards are much greater than doing it alone.

One of the most effective forms of exchange is a personal recommendation. You may not reach as many people as the Internet does through this form of exchange, but a personal recommendation from someone who knows you, has done business with you, and knows your personal work ethic is one of the most effective forms of communicating your abilities. I want to give people reasons for being able to recommend me to people they feel I can help, as will I do the same for them.

Our lives offer daily opportunities for exchanges of knowledge, information and resources. It is a perfect form of communication. Don't let any opportunity pass you by to be part of this valuable give and take.

Million-Dollar Thoughts

How many books are written on subjects that relate to your million-dollar dreams? How many have you read? Do you know less than the authors of these books? Do you at least know as much as one or two of them because you have read their works? If you haven't been reading their works, why not?

If you are to achieve your million-dollar dreams, the easiest way to begin is to learn as much as possible. The best people to learn from are those who have already succeeded in the area of your dream or are working toward it. Why start at the beginning and re-invent the wheel if you can start somewhere in the middle? Why aren't you devouring this information?

Million-Dollar Affirmation

I am learning things daily that will make my achievement of my million-dollar dreams easier.

Million-Dollar Action

Sometime this week go to the local library or bookstore. Get a book that will educate you or motivate you in an area that will help to achieve your million-dollar dreams. Then, the most important factor... read it!

Chapter 12

Million-Dollar Dreams Come True

"If one advances confidently in the direction of their dreams, and endeavors to lead a life which they have imagined, they will meet with a success unexpected in common hours."
Henry David Thoreau

In one of my sister's favorite movies, *A Walk To Remember*[7], Jamie Sullivan makes a list of 100 items that she wants to accomplish during her lifetime. These 100 items are her goals and her dreams in order to give her life meaning and direction. Some are realistic *(like reading 100 books and getting a tattoo)*, while others are seemingly impossible *(such as being in two places at the same time and to witness a miracle.)* Yet it was proved that even the seemingly impossible dreams are often possible.

Jamie knew what kind of person she wanted to be and knew what she wanted to accomplish. She was living her life intentionally, with purpose and direction. In order to achieve your million-dollar dreams, you need to do the same. You need to live your life on purpose.

Take some time and sit down and develop your own list. You will be amazed at what you find. At first it may be difficult to think of 10 things you want to accomplish, but the more you write, the clearer your thinking becomes, and ultimately you will find that you are drafting a plan for your million-dollar dreams. Why 100 items? Because successful people always do a little bit more than the next guy, and one idea can change your life. It might be number 99 or 100!

As I have said previously, you don't have to wait until a certain age to begin moving in the direction of your dreams. You can start now. Men and women who achieve their million-dollar dreams come in all ages, shapes, and sizes. And often they are no more talented than you and me. Exceptional results are often achieved by average people. The difference is:

◆ They develop their potential to the fullest. *"If we did all the things we are capable of, we would literally astound ourselves."* Thomas Edison

◆ They let their imagination run wild. *"Imagination is more important than knowledge."* Albert Einstein

◆ They believe in their dreams. *"The future belongs to those who believe in the beauty of their dreams."* Eleanor Roosevelt

◆ They dream big. *"He that believes in me, the works which I do shall he do also, and he shall do greater than these."* Jesus

◆ They think positive. *"A positive attitude is a person's passport to a better tomorrow."* Anonymous

◆ They take risks. *"Only those who will risk going too far can possibly find out how far one can go."* T. S. Eliot

◆ They have the courage to pursue their dreams. *"Courage is not the absence of fear, but rather the judgment that something else is more important than fear."* Ambrose Redmoon

◆ They prepare. *"You hit homeruns not by chance but by preparation."* Roger Maris

◆ They never give up. *"I am not the smartest or the most talented person in the world, but I succeeded because I keep going, and going, and going."* Sylvester Stallone

H.G. Wells stated, *"There is no upper limit to what individuals are capable of doing with their minds. There is no age limit that bars them from beginning. There is no obstacle that cannot be overcome if they persist and believe."* You are capable of achieving your million-dollar dreams at any age so long as you do the things necessary. No one begins life with all the tools needed to succeed, but those tools are available. It is simply up to you to discover them, develop them and put them to use.

I believe that if you read this book you are at a crossroads in your life—one that will lead to great success if you choose it. You are one-of-a-kind, unique, and have an important purpose for your life. It's just a matter of reaching out for it, believing in it, and moving toward it.

It is my hope that you now *want* to pursue your dreams. Oliver Wendell Holmes once said, *"Man's mind, stretched to a new idea, never goes back to its original dimension."* I'm hoping this book has stretched your thinking a bit so that there is no choice *but* to move forward toward your dreams. So I'm asking you to embark on a journey that will be exciting and challenging and lead you to greater successes than you have previously imagined. It's time to find out who you are and what you are capable of doing. It's time to be the best that you can be, and to achieve your *Million-Dollar Dreams.*

Million-Dollar Affirmation

I am achieving my million-dollar dreams!

Million-Dollar Action

List 100 goals and dreams.

1. _____
2. _____
3. _____
4. _____
5. _____
6. _____
7. _____
8. _____
9. _____
10. _____
11. _____
12. _____
13. _____
14. _____
15. _____
16. _____
17. _____
18. _____
19. _____
20. _____

21. _____
22. _____
23. _____
24. _____
25. _____
26. _____
27. _____
28. _____
29. _____
30. _____
31. _____
32. _____
33. _____
34. _____
35. _____
36. _____
37. _____
38. _____
39. _____
40. _____
41. _____
42. _____
43. _____
44. _____
45. _____
46. _____
47. _____
48. _____
49. _____

50. _____
51. _____
52. _____
53. _____
54. _____
55. _____
56. _____
57. _____
58. _____
59. _____
60. _____
61. _____
62. _____
63. _____
64. _____
65. _____
66. _____
67. _____
68. _____
69. _____
70. _____
71. _____
72. _____
73. _____
74. _____
75. _____
76. _____
77. _____
78. _____

79. _____
80. _____
81. _____
82. _____
83. _____
84. _____
85. _____
86. _____
87. _____
88. _____
89. _____
90. _____
91. _____
92. _____
93. _____
94. _____
95. _____
96. _____
97. _____
98. _____
99. _____
100. _____

Epilogue

At this point some of you may ask me, *have you achieved all your million-dollar dreams yet?* The honest answer is that I'm still working on them. But what you have to keep in mind is that it isn't all about the end-result. It's all about the journey - the process that takes you there. Life isn't only about achieving a goal. It's about having a dream that will give direction to your life. You don't want to live your entire life aimlessly, hoping to stumble on a path that will lead to your dreams. You need to choose the paths you take.

I wrote this book for young people, like me, because we have our whole lives ahead of us. We aren't already 50 or 60 years old looking back regretfully wishing we had pursued our dreams and lived our lives differently. We have the opportunity right now to create the life we want - to choose our own paths. This is what achieving your *Million-Dollar Dreams* is all about.

Yes, I had the dream of becoming a major league baseball player for the Boston Red Sox. I also dreamed of what it would feel like to stand in the batter's box waiting for the right pitch, and then be able to swing my bat, connect with the ball, and hit a home run over the green monster in Fenway Park. While my injury may have prevented me from becoming the major league player that I had hoped, I was given the chance to hit that home run. On July 17, 2004 I attended a fundraising event at Fenway. I stood at home plate ready and waiting for the right pitch, and when it came, I hit it. I watched it sail over the green monster and out of Fenway. I had just achieved <u>one</u> of my Million-Dollar Dreams.

Life is like a game of baseball. Sometimes you hit home runs. Sometimes you strike out. But in order to score runs, you have to follow the path that will get you to home plate. First you must follow the bases from first, to second, to third, and ultimately to home where your goal is achieved. Examine the path that you are following. Is it a path to your dreams and goals, or are you running around aimlessly in the outfield somewhere? Now is the time to choose your path.

I wish you all the best of luck in achieving your dreams; but even more, I wish you all happiness while pursuing them.

Kris

About The Author

Kris Vigue, age 21, has been an entrepreneur since the age of 12 when he began his own Internet trading-card business. He built his company over the years, and in 2003 was recognized as *NetPro* Trading Card's largest distributor worldwide.

While playing college baseball in 2002 Kris dislocated his shoulder, shattering his million-dollar dream of playing professional baseball. As a result, he brought his business million-dollar dreams to the forefront and founded *AthleteSuccess.com*, a sports motivational company to help athletes in their careers.

Kris is also a private investor. He is one of the founding investors in *The Executive Sports Club of Orlando*, a club for area business people and former and current professional athletes, and he is an investor and working partner of *Peak Power Marketing & Management*. In 2004 Kris became a licensed Athlete Agent and formed an alliance with *Legends Management Group*. He also continues to pursue his B.A. in Finance at the University of Central Florida.

To contact Kris, write to: Kris Vigue, 1004 Ridge Pointe Cove, Longwood, FL 32750

Or e-mail him at: kvigue@aol.com

Notes

[1] Paraphrased from Frederick Langbridge quote

[2] Time Bank
http://www.geocities.com/Heartland/Prairie/9743/time.htm

[3] Science For Success
http://www.scienceforsuccess.com

[4] Life Excellence
http://letters.webvalence.com/sites/LifeExcellence/Broadcast.
D20010411.html

[5] HongKong.com
http://english.hongkong.com/chain_email/shake_it_off.html

[6] Infoplease A-Z Dictionary
http://www.infoplease.com/ipd/A0551617.html

[7] Based on the book, *A Walk To Remember*, by Nicholas Sparks

You can contact Pat Williams at:

Pat Williams
c/o Orlando Magic
8701 Maitland Summit Boulevard
Orlando, FL 32810
Phone (407) 916-2404
pwilliams@orlandomagic.com

Visit Pat Williams' web site at:
www.patwilliamsmotivate.com

If you would like to set up a speaking engagement for Pat Williams, please write his assistant, Diana Basch, at the above address or call her at (407) 916-2454. Requests can be faxed to (407) 916-2986 or e-mailed to dbasch@orlandomagic.com.

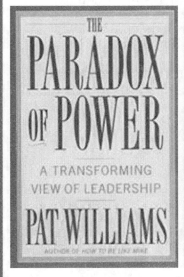

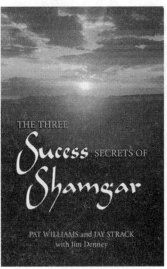

Pat Williams' books can be purchased at
www.patwilliamsmotivate.com or your local bookstore

All proceeds from sales of this book go toward college scholarships.

To apply for a chance at receiving one of these scholarships simply submit the following information along with an essay *(of no more than 500 words)* telling me how this book has encouraged you to pursue your Million-Dollar Dreams!

Send it to:
Million-Dollar Dream Scholarships
1004 Ridge Pointe Cove
Longwood, FL 32750

- -

Name: _____
Address: _____
City: _____ **State:** _____ **ZIP:** _____
E-Mail: _____

College Information:

Name of College: _____
Address: _____
City: _____ **State:** _____ **ZIP:** _____
Year _____ **Degree** _____ **Major** _____

ORDER FORM

To order additional copies of *How To Achieve Your Million-Dollar Dreams At Any Age* use the form below.

Ordered by: (please print)
Name_____
Address _____
City _____ State _____
Zip Code _____ Tel. _____

Ship to: (if different from above)
Name_____
Address _____
City _____ State _____
Zip Code _____ Tel. _____

_____ copies @ $12.95 (U.S.) _____

Payment Method:
___ Check ___ MC ___ VISA ___ AMEX ___ Discover
(Checks are payable to Power Publications, Inc.)

Credit Card # _____
Exp Date _____ 3 Digit CV# (on back of card) _____
Signature _____

Fax To: 407-261-0278 or
Mail to: Power Publications, Inc.
1004 Ridge Pointe Cove, Longwood, FL 32750

To order by phone and pay be credit card,
Call Power Publications at 1-888-895-2961.
(Call for quantity discounts)